The V woman

Cristiane Cardoso

The V woman

1st edition

Rio de Janeiro
2011

C268w

Cardoso, Cristiane
    The V-woman — Cristiane Cardoso
Rio de Janeiro : Unipro Editora, 2011.
320 p. ; 18,5 cm.

ISBN 978-85-7140-645-2

1. Woman — stage and worth.
2. Appearance — dignity.
I. Title

                                        CDD 261.5

Copyright ©2011

GENERAL COORDINATION: Carlos Macedo

EDITORIAL COORDINATION: Renato Cardoso

EDITING: Sandra Gouvêa, Evelyn Higginbotham and Chris Boodram

COVER DESIGN: Welison Calandria

COVER ART: Alexandre Coutinho and Marcelo Bento

COVER: Rafael Brum

LAYOUT. Vanessa Ferreira

PRINTED AND BOUND BY: Clays Ltd, St Ives plc

1st edition • 2011

Estrada Adhemar Bebiano, 3.610
Inhaúma – CEP: 20766-720
Rio de Janeiro – RJ – Brazil
Tel.: (+55 21) 3296-9300
editora@unipro.com.br
www.unipro.com.br

The V-Woman
Ordering code: 645-2
Caixa Postal: 264
Rio de Janeiro - RJ
CEP: 20001-970

Contents

Acknowledgments

To my Lord and Savior, who has been my Source and Inspiration, and to everyone He has used to bless me throughout my life - especially those who helped me publish this book. You know who you are.

Cristiane Cardoso

Introduction

long, long time ago, women were respected and honored. In fact, man's reputation relied on marrying a lady. We used to be a prize to be conquered.

The way we dressed, spoke, and behaved said it all. We were exclusive. We used to be attractive because of our discretion, not because of our clothes.

Sure many will say that women from the past didn't have much of what we have today, and they're right; but one thing they had that we lack today is value. They were valued.

We may have conquered a lot in the past decades, but we've also lost a lot; and just as when something loses its value, it becomes cheap, common, and disregarded, many of us feel exactly the same way.

The woman

A Women have lost their female essence, the beauty they used to carry just by the way they moved. For some reason, beauty now has completely different standards; it's about the looks.

If you don't look right, you're not beautiful. The beauty industry (yes, there's an industry) teaches people not to care about who they are, the person beneath the skin. And for this reason, you only feel really valued when you're looking attractive; and since we all know looks don't last, age sucks out all that value until you feel worthless and forgotten.

Isn't that what happens all the time before the world's eyes? Celebrities that used to be loved and admired are quickly forgotten as they grow old or gain weight. Other celebrities focus on doing a lot of charitable works so they won't be loved only by what they mean to the media, but for the things they've done... but they too are forgotten, they too suffer the consequences of being devalued.

...since we all know looks don't last, age sucks out all that value...

Their husbands don't think twice about having an affair; their children can't wait to leave home; their so-called friends spread gossip about them; their relatives run their shadow hoping to feed off their success; and then there are the fans who feel disappointed in them for something they said. So much for being a celebrity.

If the women who are most loved and talked about in the world are treated this way, what about the rest of us? What's wrong with women these days? Why, after so much that we've conquered for ourselves, are we still trying to conquer the one thing we search for the most?

Men have begun looking at us as objects – not as a prize as it used to be, but a burden. Many don't want to get married, they don't want to commit to one woman for the rest of their lives – it's too boring! Some commit just because they need that status in society, for the sake of their own careers.

And most of them don't even have to conquer women anymore; they can get a new one at the snap of their fingers. It seems women have lost all of their shame and self-respect. They ask men out, they let them see more than they need to, they let them do more than they have to. They let them use them for free.

And if men were the only ones looking down on women, it might even be tolerable, but women do the same. They don't help one another at all. They're always looking at each other's faults, criticizing themselves as if not on the same team. Women have been one of women's worst enemies. One of the most common things you'll find among them is gossip and criticism, and guess what about? Other women! If women can't value themselves, do you think men will?

Our small and insignificant ego is always too lazy to get up and make an appearance. If you praise a man, his ego quickly goes through the roof. If you do the same to a woman, it floats just below her head for a while and then like a balloon running out of gas, it sinks back down to the floor.

We have the media bashing us with their all-mighty-power, given by I wonder who, telling women what's beautiful and what's not. Just the icing on that depressive cake women from all over the world share daily.

No wonder they feel so low. No wonder they settle for the first guy that shows any interest.

How different today's woman has become from the original woman God created. And you may again

think of all the things we've achieved throughout history, but at what cost?

We used to be beautiful from inside out. We used to be cared for. We used to be lovely, understanding, and gentle. An incredible being whose warmth was beyond anything in this world... Our children wanted to be like us.

Today, it's almost as if we've shot ourselves in the foot. We want to do more, to be more, to give more, but at the same time, we feel the loss that comes with all that. There are more battles happening in a woman's world than anywhere else out there.

Men strive to conquer while we strive to do that and be in control. Men can still be single in their 30s and take their time, but for us, the clock is already ticking... This controlling bug can many times lead us to terrible decisions. It's fueled by all the stress we acquire from anywhere we look. It's as if everybody out there was targeting us... especially the media.

No wonder they settle for the first guy that shows any interest.

No matter how stress comes, it doesn't only come and go; it loads us up like a big truck, and as we can't stand it for too long, we vent. Vent at our loved ones, vent at strangers in traffic, and at ourselves in the mirror. Nothing is ever good enough, but how could it be? We're not good enough for ourselves.

How sad it is to see how low we've sunk, how worthless and insignificant we see ourselves, to the point of settling for less than average. We let the media tell us we're too fat, too skinny, too old-fashioned, too shy, inadequate — and that our hips are too wide. And then we take their word seriously and condemn ourselves for it. We spend everything trying to make ourselves look better and better, but they're always coming up with something new and what we have is again not good enough anymore.

Men strive to conquer while we strive to do that and be in control.

So we go and tear our own image down with whatever we can find in order to attract men. We

do anything, whatever it takes, no matter how, only to get a little attention, to be noticed, to be attractive, to be wanted, to be valued.

But that doesn't do it either. The way we dress, the way we walk, the way we speak, the way our bodies transformed against our will — everything about us is never good enough. And so we grow tired of it all… after all the failed trials, we give up, taking one day at a time until the day we finally leave this women-degrading world.

Could this be a curse we have to carry from generation to generation? The grandma suffered, the mother suffered, and the daughters are suffering… when is this going to end? Are we born to live this low? Some of us stood up for more rights, demanded to be treated equally, and achieved much, but not enough to change the way we feel about ourselves. We work double shifts every single day: the career and the looks. Without the looks, the career is limited. Without the career, the looks are limited.

It's not that it's a man's world; it's just that we are not fitting in it. Maybe we've just been working on the wrong things…

Perhaps we need to figure out who exactly we've been so we can start changing back to who we are supposed to be.

The woman

I ask, how long will women just sit there and accept all the degrading female portraits displayed everywhere in books, movies, billboards, magazines, TV, music, and fashion?

Do you want to be respected? Respect yourself first. Do you want to be valued? Value yourself first. Treat yourself well, like a lady. Do you want to attract the right man? Be the right woman for him.

Some like to say, "Men are all the same", but aren't women like that too? They're all becoming the same... displaying the same attitudes that have repeatedly proven not to work.

Tighten those clothes... be more seductive... wear less... laugh louder... be sexy... be flirty... be mysterious... be tough... be bitter... fall into a trap. Can this be the way to value oneself?

If looks were what it takes to be valued, why are all these beautiful, body-toned, sexy celebrities so unfortunate in their love lives?

As a baby, you wanted your needs to be met. As a child, you asked to be spoiled. As a teenager, you begged for attention. As a woman, you want to be valued.

Everyone wants to be valued; no matter how old they are, where they're from, or who they are.

The only way that you'll ever be valued is when you understand what true value means and how you can attain it for yourself and become a V-Woman. Now let's find out what that V stands for.

Some (women) like to say, "Men are all the same", but aren't women like that too?

The woman

My Notes

- Value Yourself First

The V-Woman

Who can find a virtuous wife? For her worth is far above rubies.

(Proverbs 31:10)

The ruby is one of the most beautiful, expensive, and rare gemstones in the world. In fact, it's considered the undisputed ruler of all gemstones, the "king of jewels".

According to a jewelry reference center, the most expensive ruby ever sold at auction was a 15.97-carat stone that sold for $3.63 million in 1988!

As with anything else in this world, the less there is of something, the more valuable it becomes, and the fewer people have it.

The value of a virtuous woman goes far and beyond physical worth; I like to

call her "the V-Woman". She goes through the same struggles as every other woman in this world, of every age, of every nation, of every background, of every circumstance, but none of those struggles diminishes her worth, unlike so many women out there.

That's why she's as rare as rubies. She's different in many ways. Her qualities and traits are rare. And yet, most women are so easily attracted to what's common, not to what's rare...

Looks are not rare – anybody can look beautiful. In fact, nowadays, models don't even have to be beautiful – Photoshop does the trick. A woman can pay the best doctors in the world for an all-over-body lift, but she can't pay to change her worth. The V-Woman, on the other hand, does not have to be rich to be priceless.

> A woman can pay the best doctors in the world for an all-over-body lift, but she can't pay to change her worth.

Financial success may not be everywhere, but it certainly isn't rare. If you apply yourself, study, work hard, and sacrifice,

you know you can be successful in whatever career you decide to pursue.

Marriage is not rare either. Anybody can get married these days. I wouldn't be surprised if online marriage became accepted one day. The holy institution of marriage has now become a joke for many. More and more people are dismissing it, preferring to shack up instead.

So what's really rare these days? A woman who is happy with herself and, as a consequence, happily married and valued by her own family.

That rarity is something you can't buy or order anywhere. It's not that it's out of stock; it's just only available for those who choose to follow the road to wisdom.

> *Wisdom calls aloud outside; she raises her voice in the open squares. She cries out in the chief concourses, at the openings of the gates in the city she speaks her words: "How long, you simple ones, will you love simplicity? For scorners delight in their scorning, and fools hate knowledge. Turn at my rebuke; surely I will pour out my spirit on you; I will make*

my words known to you. Because I have called and you refused, I have stretched out my hand and no one regarded, because you disdained all my counsel, and would have none of my rebuke, I also will laugh at your calamity; I will mock when your terror comes, when your terror comes like a storm, and your destruction comes like a whirlwind, when distress and anguish come upon you. Then they will call on me, but I will not answer; they will seek me diligently, but they will not find me. Because they hated knowledge and did not choose the fear of the LORD, they would have none of my counsel and despised my every rebuke. Therefore they shall eat the fruit of their own way, and be filled to the full with their own fancies. For the turning away of the simple will slay them, and the complacency of fools will destroy them; But whoever listens to me will dwell safely, and will be secure, without fear of evil."

(Proverbs 1:20-33)

Let's take a look at this long passage in more detail, going over the words in bold:

1. *"Wisdom calls aloud outside; she raises her voice in the open squares."* We learn that wisdom is calling out, almost as if she was shouting at the people that pass her by. She calls not just from one, but from several places.

This means wisdom is found anywhere. You don't need to be educated, knowledgeable, or go to the finest schools for that. As the verses above say, wisdom is found in quite common places. It mentions the open squares, chief concourses, and openings of the gates; in other words, wisdom is easily available. The problem is that no one is really looking for it!

If you don't see the need for something, you won't really look for it. If you think you know it all, if you're the type that has to make your own mistakes before you learn a lesson — like many young adults tell their parents — then of course, you're among the simple ones.

...means wisdom is found anywhere.

2. *"How long, you simple ones, will you love simplicity?"* The simple ones love simplicity. In the book of Proverbs, simple really means simple-minded or ignorant. The simple are complacent people who don't look for ways to become better or to do better next time. Instead, they're always repeating the same mistakes, falling into the same traps in life.

They never learn their lesson and often misunderstand what they're taught. They're "airheads" who won't take advantage of opportunities. If they lose a job, instead of looking for a better one and avoiding the same mistakes they made in their previous job, they sink into depression, complaining about the unfairness of life and living constantly in the past. They don't move on.

> The simple are complacent people who don't look for ways to become better or to do better next time.

3. *"For scorners delight in their scorning..."* Instead of learning from the mistakes of others, simple people are scorners. It's much easier to make fun

of others' failures and point fingers than to learn valuable lessons from those failures. We often see this in young adults who disrespect their parents because of all their mistakes, and yet walk down the same path to make the exact same mistakes themselves.

4. *"...and fools hate knowledge."* They hate knowledge; these people can't stand reading a book, taking the time to read the Bible, or even listening to sound advice. They'd rather listen to music, and chat and tweet every vapid thought that comes to mind. They may be going downhill, but they won't put on the brakes. They just switch into neutral and coast.

5. *"Turn at my rebuke..."* To acquire wisdom, you need to accept rebuke. There's just no other way around it. You can't really learn anything without being rebuked along the way. Remember when you first learned how to drive? How about the time when your parents rebuked you for something you said? Would you have learned your lesson if they had just politely asked you to stop? Come on! People are too sensitive to use this excuse in order to avoid a rebuke. That's why they never learn, never change, never get better.

6. *"I also will laugh at your calamity..."* Obviously, simpletons don't listen to wisdom, and so they keep on

making tons of mistakes, one after the other – wrong decisions, wrong relationships, wrong careers, wrong steps, wrong, wrong, wrong... And, in that constant state of loss, they feel they've been dealt a raw deal by the cold cruel world. Life makes fun of them and sometimes it almost feels like they're in a never-ending horror movie. With so much bad luck, they think they were born to suffer. But it's not bad luck, it's not life trying to teach them a lesson, it's nothing more than their lack of wisdom.

7. *"Then they will call on me, but I will not answer..."* So they look for wisdom but it seems too late to find it. They've made so many mistakes, made such a mess that now it seems that wisdom has left them for good. But it's not about missing an opportunity and never having it again, but more about lacking the fear of God. The Bible constantly attributes the first as a consequence of the latter. You just can't be wise without the fear of God. A lot of people look for wisdom and they can't find it, and won't ever find it, without seeking God first.

8. *"Therefore they shall eat the fruit of their own way..."* Every action has a corresponding reaction. If you sow bad seed, you'll reap bad fruit. I get really

fed up of hearing people complain that if God existed, there would be no suffering in this world. People make bad choices and blame God for their misfortune, as if He made them do it. So you married a guy who was an alcoholic and now he abuses you – where is God? You slept with your boyfriend and now that you're pregnant, he doesn't want anything to do with you or the baby – where is God? You yell at your daughter all day long, for everything and anything, and now that she hates your guts and is moving out, you ask "where is God?"… Now, I ask, where is your common sense?

9. *"…and the complacency of fools will destroy them…"* CComplacency is the result. People often realize they made mistakes and that they should have done this or that. But though they know all the lessons they should apply in the future, instead of doing something about it, they're complacent. They get used to their life of failure, of just getting by, too lazy to get up and change things for the better. They prefer the comfort of their chair and a computer on their lap. All

You just can't be wise without the fear of God.

The V-woman

they ask for is some kind of distraction that will last long enough so they won't have to think about where their life is headed.

10. *"But whoever listens to me will dwell safely, and will be secure, without fear of evil."* For anyone to listen to wisdom talking, they need to think. No one can actively listen without thinking. The beauty of this passage in the Bible, in fact everything about God for that matter, is that there's always an exit, a way out. God always gives us another chance and when we finally take it, our future changes. We no longer need to fear or avoid our future; we look forward to it because it's from God Himself.

The V-Woman's secret lies right there. She's worth more than rubies because she's virtuous. She's virtuous because she makes the right decisions in life. She makes the right decisions in life because she listens to wisdom. She listens to wisdom because she fears God.

...too lazy to get up and change things for the better.

When your worth is more than rubies, you

don't need to settle for less. You're one-of-a-kind. Just as there are many women, there are many gemstones, some are rarer than others, but the ruby… the ruby is THE gemstone!

I don't think it's a coincidence that the Bible mentions rubies when talking about wisdom and women. According to God, the three are related. Check these verses below:

> *No mention shall be made of coral or quartz, for the price of wisdom is above rubies.*

(Job 28:18)

(This verse below is a female personification of wisdom. How interesting!)

> *She is more precious than rubies, and all the things you may desire cannot compare with her. Length of days is in her right hand, in her left hand riches and honor. Her ways are ways of pleasantness, and all her paths are peace. She is a tree of life to those who take hold of her, and happy are all who retain her.*

(Proverbs 3:15-18)

For wisdom is better than rubies, and all the things one may desire cannot be compared with her.

(Proverbs 8:11)

And our own V-Woman one:

Who can find a virtuous wife? For her worth is far above rubies.

(Proverbs 31:10)

Rubies, wisdom, and women are somehow related in the Bible. Who can find them? Who? The question is not where they are or how we can find them, but who can find them? Who? You! The V-Woman wasn't just one person long, long ago, nor is the V-Woman just some single person that exists today. The V-Woman can be you!

It doesn't matter where you're from, what you've been through, and how you've lived your life until today. What matters is that you, the 'who' in question, are looking; and if you look, you'll find.

Each of the following chapters in this book is dedicated to one verse in Proverbs 31, all about the V-Woman. And each verse describes one quality she possesses that can be easily included in your own set of qualities, showing you how to become a V-Woman by the end of this book. There's no out-of-this-world wisdom here, just plain straight to the point guidelines; and if you go ahead and do them, they can change you and your family dramatically.

Let's begin.

> The V-Woman wasn't just one person long, long ago... The V-Woman can be you!

The woman

My Notes

- Rubies – Valuable
- The less of a thing the more valuable
- Don't have to be rich to be priceless

Prov. 1:20-33 – Wisdom is to be found

You cannot be wise without the fear of God

She's trusted

The heart of her husband safely trusts her; so he will have no lack of gain.

(Proverbs 31:11)

*I*n the verse above, you can see the relationship between trust and money quite clearly. The husband's heart, where all his emotions of worries, concern, fear, and doubts come from, safely trusts her with money; as if to say he's not worried about her ability to use their family's income. She's responsible, she's mature.

Trust is about maturity and responsibility. You can't trust someone who's not mature because you know that person won't make sound decisions. An immature woman often doesn't know how to handle responsibilities and spends her money based on her feelings rather than on sound principles.

It's unbelievable how many young women don't want to grow up and become mature. In fact, sometimes it feels as though they work hard to NOT mature. They want to speak and behave the same way, as if that could stop time and cause them to remain teenagers forever.

Obviously whoever thinks that way can never be the virtuous woman of Proverbs 31 – it's about a virtuous woman, not a virtuous girl. The Bible often speaks of women of God, never girls of God, because there's just no such thing. When you meet God, you grow up. You never stay the same, you see things differently, you become a whole new you.

Maturity makes you think of the consequences of your actions. You no longer act or speak by impulse or by the emotions you feel at the moment. Instead, you think of what those actions could lead you to. Imagine if every young woman thought about the consequences of her choices? One thing

Maturity makes you think of the consequences of your actions.

is for sure: that would put an end to the problem of teenage pregnancy!

When you don't think for yourself, someone else does it for you – and that's how you're enslaved. You're enslaved in a life with all the wrong kinds of relationships and an aimless future you'll most certainly regret.

If people are going to trust you, they need to see that you think for yourself. You wouldn't trust anyone who is gullible and easily influenced by others, would you?

Common belief holds that. You need people to start trusting you so you can build up trust. But the truth is that it all starts with you. If you want to be trusted, do what it takes. Be responsible. Be mature. Think.

The V-Woman's husband trusts her because he knows he can. A trustworthy woman does not need to convince anyone that they can trust her; her daily behavior says it all. You can tell when someone is mature just by the way they speak. They're confident enough to look in your eyes when speaking to you. They may be shy but they do what they have to; they're responsible with their obligations.

That's why the V-Woman lacks nothing nor does she let her family lack. She thinks of herself and her

family as one. If her family is struggling financially, she doesn't just hope for the best – she provides them with hope.

It's never about her own plans, her own desires, and her own life. And for this, her husband trusts her. He feels secure that they're both in the same boat and he's not the only one rowing . His wife doesn't only prioritize their family's needs but also saves – something out of this world for many women.

Perhaps the media is to blame, as they make us always feel inadequate about what we wear and how we look. Most commercials are targeted at us because they know we're easily influenced by them. Let's be honest; with a few exceptions, women like to spend!

Few people save money these days. We're becoming more and more of a shopaholic society. The more gadgets they sell, the more junk we fill our homes with – even in a recession! That's amazing.

Fashion is another major reason for this. It brainwashes us through the media to the point of making us look at our full closet and think, "I have nothing to wear today."

The V-Woman saves money. She has a savings account and, though she spends some on herself, there's always some left to earn interest. It's not always because she wants to buy something later, many times it's just to save for a rainy day. If there's an emergency, her family won't go without. Again, only people who think ahead do this – maturity is a need, not a commodity.

Now here's a statement you may hate me for, but please bear with me and you will understand why: A mature woman enjoys growing old.

She understands that, in order to become better, she needs time. You can't really mature in mere days. So why is growing old so underrated? When you grow old, you live life to the full. How could that be a problem?

Again, our society is too focused on the physical, on how we look, when in fact, there's nothing we

> The V-Woman saves money... has a savings account and, though she spends some on herself, there's always some left to earn interest..

can do about that except to accept our aging. It's just part of life. No mother-to-be complains about child-birth, exactly because she knows that it's just part of what she has to go through in order to have a baby.

Maturity can be achieved by growing old. Life experience opens our eyes and makes us more mature, more adult, and even more feminine.

There's nothing better for our own inner-self than growing older. We learn, we change, and we become better women in so many ways. But that is not the only way to achieve maturity.

Another way is how you handle your responsibilities. Everybody has them, no matter how old they are. Even a four-year-old does – for example, when asked to draw something in class on the first day at school.

When you're not responsible, you show you're not mature enough... you're not trusted with much.

You may be given a responsibility, but that doesn't mean you're responsible. And that's the big difference. When

you're not responsible, you show you're not mature enough and, consequently, you're not trusted with much.

Responsibility means you were found worthy of taking care of something, and not just anything, but something that means a lot, something that not everyone has the privilege of doing or caring for. Whenever you're given a responsibility, your immediate feeling is always positive. It becomes a "Yes, they believe in me!" moment.

In school, when you were told to help someone else; at home, when you were asked to cook a certain night of the week; at work, when you were trusted with something new; in church, when someone confided in you with their problems – these were all tests in how you handled responsibility.

And through each test, some are given more and others lose the little they have. It's not a game, it's life. Once you show yourself to be irresponsible, it's like you've glued a sign onto your forehead announcing "untrustworthy".

As important as it is to be found responsible, it's also important how you handle losing a responsibility. Yes, it's another kind of test. If you're just "okay" with

it, it says a whole lot about you:"I didn't care about it anyway. Thanks for taking that burden off my shoulders. I don't want any more responsibilities, thanks."

It's quite common to see few people trusted with much and most people trusted with little. The small group of people that take their responsibilities seriously are usually given more, to the point they're overloaded, while the large group of people that are not trusted with much hardly have anything to do. These are often the ones who get involved in gossip, because they just have too much time on their hands. Immature people like to gossip, they don't like to work with deadlines, and they love their spare time.

Your maturity goes hand in hand with your responsibilities. The more responsibilities you have, the more mature you are, and the more trusted you will be. Now read that again, this time in the negative: The fewer responsibilities you have, the less mature you are, and the less trusted you will be.

Few women come to their senses regarding this. Most of the rest keep on blaming others because they feel shut out: "So and so doesn't like me, that's why I'm never chosen" or "So and so thinks I'm not good enough".

If you're not responsible, of course you're not good enough.

I think we can easily compare the sense of trust to when you lend something you really like to someone. In the back of your mind, you're afraid you'll never see it again, and even though you don't need it urgently, you wish the person would return it to you promptly. But there are those people who don't, who often forget to return things lent to them. Just the fact that you have to remind them is already a reason you have to never ever lend them anything from then on. But when the person quickly returns it to you, you feel as though you can trust her with more, that she has proven herself responsible enough to be "lend-worthy."

I think that being responsible begins with the very basic responsibilities we all have, which can be very obvious to others and not so obvious to ourselves. These are the things in life that only you can do. You can't

As important as it is to be found responsible, it's also important how you handle losing a responsibility.

The woman

wait on others, you can't depend on others, you just have to go and do them. For instance, here's a list of a few of them:

- **Take care of your health** — eat right, exercise, and take good care of yourself; after all, if you're sick, how will you ever do anything else?

- **Take care of your spiritual life** — pray, read the Bible, keep your heart clean, and attend church. People lack faith in God because they simply ignore these basic spiritual needs. Without your faith, you can't go very far, and the place you end up in won't be the place that you want to be.

- **Give of yourself** — nobody can do it for you. If you keep on waiting to receive before you give to others, you might as well just lie down and wait for the nails in your coffin.

- **Be yourself** — only you can do that! So why keep on trying to be someone else? It's like having a rip-off copy of the real thing. How cheap!

> If you keep on waiting to receive before you give to others, you might as well just lie down and wait for the nails in your coffin.

• **Be aware of others' expectations of you** — whatever post you've been given in life, do it well. If you're a mother, daughter, employee, wife, homemaker, or student, know this: only you can be what you're called to be. The positions are yours – don't neglect them. Fulfill them well.

Many times, the missing piece in a young woman's life is maturity. She dresses, speaks, and lives like older women, but she's not responsible with the little she has. Her mind is too absorbed with everything else instead of her own responsibilities before people and God. Disappointment and hardship are always at her doorstep.

The older we get, the wiser we become, the fewer mistakes we make, and the more we're trusted.

YOUNG AND INEXPERIENCED

Mary was a young virgin when the Angel of the Lord appeared to her to give her the best news she had ever received – she was going to give birth to the Son of God!

One wonders why God chose her out of all the other young virgins in Israel at the time. Mary was

trusted with the most important task in the world: be the mother of our Lord Jesus. She must have had something other young women her age didn't...

You can imagine how young and inexperienced Mary was at this stage in her life – she wasn't even married yet. But instead of asking how, when, why, what, and panicking about the risk this would mean for her own life, she gladly accepted the challenge.

Mary wasn't necessarily ready for that challenge, but she trusted that God would give her what she needed to become ready. God trusted her because she trusted Him.

People say they believe in God, but few people actually trust Him with their lives. Mary was going to risk being stoned to death for showing up pregnant before her wedding day, and yet she trusted God would take care of her. If she could trust in God, she could be trusted with His Son.

When you can finally stop trusting in your own strength and start trusting in God with your life, issues, problems, difficulties, and concerns, you mature.

God looks for women who can trust Him wholeheartedly so He can make a difference in the world

through them. They are women who are responsible with their faith in Him. They don't compromise; they live what they preach.

I remember a husband who couldn't celebrate his wife's achievements at work because of the high price he was paying for it at home. She was always too busy with work to take care of his things; always in a rush, hardly ever taking care of her own looks. One day, her husband demanded that she leave her very prominent career or else she could forget about their marriage. She came to speak to me with tears in her eyes, feeling horrible at his latest demand. She felt he didn't love her enough to put up with all her responsibilities outside home, but I had to tell her the truth…

He was right. Her career had taken most of her time, which really meant first place in her life. Anything that takes most of your time has to be considered the most important thing in your life, it

> The older we get, the wiser we become, the fewer mistakes we make, and the more we're trusted.

The woman

doesn't matter how you feel about it — it's a fact. In order for her to save her marriage, she had to go back to the drawing board and focus on her first most basic responsibilities that no one else could do for her.

Think with me. Could any other woman do what she did at work? Yes, of course! But no other woman could ever do what she wasn't doing for her husband at home. No wonder he felt neglected, no wonder he found it hard to appreciate all her hard earned money. He was paying a high price for it!

This woman decided to focus on her marriage and put all her other responsibilities on standby. A few months later, not only was she happier in her marriage, but she was also trusted with more than she had ever had before.

> Anything that takes most of your time has to be considered the most important thing in your life...

She may have been mature at work, but she wasn't mature enough at home. What's the use? If

you can't be trusted at home, what is the point of being trusted anywhere else?

If you trust in God and do the things only you can do, He honors you, and He doesn't take long to do it.

Ask yourself these questions:

"Can you be trusted at this moment of your life?"

"Why/Why not?"

"Who trusts you?"

"What can you start doing to increase people's trust in you?"

"How about God's?"

My Notes

She's good

She does him good and not evil all the days of her life.

(Proverbs 31:12)

Everyone wants to be happy. Everyone searches for something that can bring them happiness. But not everyone knows how much happiness depends on oneself. You can often hear single women say how much they want to be married one day and be happy, but you won't hear them say how much they want to marry one day so that they can make a man happy.

It's always about us, our own happiness, our own plans and desires, our own life. We won't admit it, but when problems come, it becomes clear that it was all about us from the beginning. And then it's hard to swallow our pride and just change.

The V woman

The V-Woman does good to everyone around her. She doesn't bring them shame, she doesn't get them in trouble, and she doesn't harm them in any way.

Many women don't understand what true friendship is all about. They think it's about having someone to talk to, someone to vent their frustrations to, someone to lean on; when, in fact, it should be the other way around. It's about being someone to talk to, being there for others to vent at when they need, to be someone others can lean on.

This is why people become so disappointed with life. They keep waiting for others to do what they should be doing in the first place. It's just so much easier to put the blame on others... I've lost count of how many times I've come across statements such as, "there are no real friends out there", "don't count on anyone, nobody cares about you", and "people are all the same".

> This is why people become so disappointed with life. They keep waiting for others to do what they should be doing in the first place.

Whenever I hear people say they don't have friends, I can't help but think that they're not real friends themselves. When you behave as a true friend towards others, you make friends. When you don't, you don't make them either.

Proverbs 31:12 doesn't say that he does her good first and so she does him good all the days of her life. It just mentions her doing good, for a reason. The Bible is revealing here how a woman like you and me can be virtuous. What we need others to be for us, we should be first. Give what we want from others. Do what we expect in others.

Once someone asked me a tricky question about friendship. She found out that her best friend's husband was cheating on her and her friend didn't have a clue about it. She asked me if she should tell her friend and break her heart, or simply let her friend find out on her own. I then asked her what she'd want her friend to do if she was the one being cheated on.

It's so much easier to deal with people around us when we start putting ourselves in their shoes. What would we want people to do, or say? How would we want them to behave? That's what we should do then!

If you heard gossip about your friend, don't go and blab it to her without any regard to what that gossip will cost her. It's better not to know that someone dislikes us than to know it. A true friend spares you from gossip and unnecessary information that can cause you to hold a grudge in your heart. But if there is important information that is crucial for her to know, even if it may upset her, you have to be friend enough to tell her and be prepared to be the one to comfort and encourage her to make the right decision. A wise woman knows the difference between foolish gossip and serious issues.

Many people also misuse doing good to others as a way to get something in return. Whether they're doing good to be recognized or to get some kind of reward, they're not really doing good to anyone but themselves. The V-Woman does good for the sake of others, not herself.

She gives for the pleasure of giving, not for the pleasure of receiving later. She's a true friend even to those who don't appreciate her. Her goodness does not depend on other people's goodness – which seems to be the trend these days.

I remember counseling two married women who shared one small house with their husbands. They

were both missionaries in Africa and they weren't related to each other in any way, apart from being colleagues in the ministry. Their problem at first seemed to be because they didn't talk to each other. The house felt more like a hotel than anything else. They'd leave home early in the morning, spend the whole day in church, and come back only late at night just to go straight to bed. There was no communication between them, which led one to assume things about the other.

As I started to ask them questions about how things like cooking and cleaning were organized in the house, they quickly replied that they didn't have a problem with that because each one had her own space in the fridge, the cabinets, and each one had her own cleaning day. Basically, they did everything separately, including the cooking, to the point that each one threw away her own trash in her own can in the kitchen.

They lived separate lives inside the same house and didn't realize that there lay the root

Many people also misuse doing good to others as a way to get something in return.

of their problems. They were having problems being friends with each other because they weren't doing what friends do. Friends share. Friends help one another. Friends don't separate food in the fridge with a name tag!

When I asked why they did it, one of them told me it was because that's how things were the minute she moved in with the other one, so she just followed the routine of the house.

Basically, she changed what she felt was right so she could follow someone else's limitations. She stopped doing good to others because she was now living with someone who wasn't in the mood to return kindness.

We should never depend on others to do good; otherwise, we'll never really succeed at it. We must do good regardless of what others do or don't do.

Friends help one another. Friends don't separate food in the fridge with a name tag!

After they followed my advice about shop-

ping, cooking, and cleaning together, their relationship evolved into a good friendship and they no longer lived like strangers in the house. They even stopped missing their families and friends back home because they had learned to build one of their own.

UNLOVED AND UNATTRACTIVE

Leah married Jacob against his will and, a week later, he married his true love Rachel, leading Leah to be his neglected other wife. Now, besides the fact that her younger sister had always been more beautiful, Rachel also had their husband's heart.

It must have been hard for Leah, living in a marriage where she felt excluded and unloved; an unnecessary extra. But even in the middle of all that suffering, Leah never stopped loving Jacob and, because of that, God blessed her with many children.

With every child Leah bore, she praised God and wished Jacob would start loving her more. But for a very long time, he didn't.

Rachel was quite the opposite of Leah, besides the fact that she had the exclusive love of their husband and the great looks. She didn't fear God; instead, she

The V-woman

lived her life competing against her older sister, as if there was anything to compete for. All that Leah had were children of her own, and still Rachel envied the little she had.

Leah had all the reasons to despise Rachel, but it was the other way around. Leah was good-hearted; she was the one who bore Judah, whose line our Savior the Lord Jesus was born into.

When Leah died, she was buried in the family tomb in Hebron, along with Abraham, Sarah, Isaac, Rebecca, and Jacob. When Rachel died giving birth, she was buried on the way to Bethlehem. The fact that the Bible mentions this little detail says a lot about both women. Both were married to Jacob, God's chosen, but only one of them, the one with the plain looks, the one Jacob loved less, was God's true choice.

The one who had it all didn't have it all, after all! The one who had nothing did have it all. Leah was a good woman; she appreciated her husband even without his love in return. She didn't turn against God because of all her misfortunes, unlike Rachel.

Leah was a V-Woman and, if Jacob had given her the love she was due, he would have struggled less in

his life. Leah also put herself in Jacob's shoes; she understood why he didn't love her as much as Rachel, and that didn't keep her from giving him her love. She still appreciated every little bit he gave her. And instead of doing what some women would in her shoes, she kept pleasing him, regardless of how unwanted he made her feel.

The V-Woman is good regardless of who is good, and who is not.

So many wives fall into this trap of doing their husbands some good only when their husbands do good to them first. I often hear the same thing over and over again when counseling married women.

"My husband doesn't fulfill my needs", "My husband doesn't understand me", "My husband doesn't help me"... me, me, me... it always ends with me. I know exactly how they feel because that's something I went through in the beginning of my marriage and, just

> Leah had all
> the reasons to
> despise Rachel,
> but it was the
> other way around.

like them, I'd always complain about something my husband didn't do for me.

It was all about my needs. I was home most of the week and, when he spent time at home, he wanted to rest while I wanted to go out. I used to feel caged in my own house. My husband, on the other hand, saw our house as a comforting home to relax in instead. He'd spend most of the week in church and so the house meant "time out" for him.

But I wouldn't let him have his time out. I'd nag him all day long if I had to, if it wasn't with my words, it was with my actions: "I'm not cooking dinner Saturday night! I've cooked all week long, I'm tired!"

While I focused on my need to be appreciated by him, I didn't notice his needs and, even worse, I criticized him for it. No wonder we had many problems in the first few years of our marriage. We were only a happy couple when things were going my way — we women are

> While I focused on my need to be appreciated by him, I didn't notice his needs...

experts at this. If things are the way we want them to be, we're happy. If they're not, we're grumpy and let everyone know it. Meanwhile, husbands just tolerate it, give in, or shut down altogether. My husband would shut down. He'd give me the silent treatment.

We don't even realize that, while we're complaining or explaining why we're upset, we're also nagging. We nag because we think if we are not heard, things won't change; and if we don't speak on and on, we think they won't do anything about it. But haven't we been proven wrong already by now? Nagging, complaining, or constant explaining (whatever you want to call it) does not change things.

Things can only change when we start changing. When we stop thinking about our needs and start thinking about our husband's needs, a miracle happens: our husbands start changing without us telling them to!

That's exactly what happened to me. After years of prayers and using every kind of manipulative method I could find, I decided to change. I stopped demanding to be fulfilled and started fulfilling my husband's needs. If he wanted to stay home, I'd stay home with a pleasant attitude and without the typical long face. I'd sit next to him and watch his favorite soccer TV channel, even though I hadn't the slightest apprecia-

tion for it. He'd ask me what I wanted to do that day, and instead of demanding my way, I'd say, "Let's do whatever you want today."

I'm not going to lie and say this change was easy, but it was totally doable. I did it and it didn't take too long before my husband started doing the things I used to beg him to, but this time without me having to say a word! Of his own will, he'd take me out, and he'd choose a movie he knew I'd like to watch.

I changed and then he changed. That is always going to be the order of things, whether you need a change in your marriage or a change in your family — you change first.

Don't wait for your husband or your mother, father, child, or boss to change so you can change. Become a better you, treat them the way you'd like them to treat you. Do them good every day, not just for a week or two. At first, they might even think you're up to something and they'll doubt your real motives, but once they see that you've changed for good, they'll have no other choice but to change themselves. As my husband often says, the spotlight will be on them.

And the great thing about this is that anyone can do it!

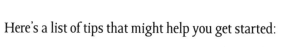

Here's a list of tips that might help you get started:

• Put yourself in that person's shoes and you'll know exactly what she or he needs from you.

• Don't take too long to do something for others that you could easily do today.

• If what you're going to say is not necessary information and may wound someone's heart and faith, don't say it.

• If you have something you can do without, and you know someone who needs it, then give it away.

• You don't always have to have something to say, but you should always have an ear to listen.

• Do what that person needs from you, not what you feel like doing for that person.

Read this again:

> *"She does him good and not evil all the days of her life"*
>
> (Proverbs 31:12)

Don't wait for your husband or your mother, father, child, or boss to change so you can change.

The woman

All the days of her life. Not just today or tomorrow, but from now on.

Do you know anyone who is going through a hard time?

What could you do for him or her that you would like done if you were in their shoes?

How can you be genuinely good to this person?

My Notes

She's hard-working

She seeks wool and flax, and willingly works with her hands.

(Proverbs 31:13)

One of the ugliest things a woman can be is lazy, and she knows it. Laziness makes us feel bad about ourselves, and we usually take it out on others around us. Things don't work as they should, time goes by too quickly, things are left undone, and suddenly we're yelling at our kids, being rude to the cashier, and rolling our eyes when our boss turns his back. We not only infuriate everyone around us, we infuriate ourselves because we know that, deep down, it's all our fault. We could have done more but we decided to be lazy.

No one respects a lazy person; no one listens to what a lazy person has to say.

They're looked down upon — it's a fact. They're just not good enough for highly trusted positions.

Laziness is not only related to work, it's related to everything we do. The way we take care of ourselves, our looks and our health. The time we wake up in the morning and start our day. The way our room or our house looks. How we behave at school or work. Basically, everything about us says that either we're hard workers or lazy.

People often attribute their laziness to a lack of time. They say they don't have time to take care of everything, but if you followed that person around 24 hours a day, you'd find where her time is usually being wasted: she takes too long to get things done, she doesn't work hard to finish her tasks, she's usually slow and easily distracted. Twenty-four hours is never enough for a lazy person.

Some blame their laziness on others. They depend too much on people in order to get things done. The

> Basically, everything about us says that either we're hard workers or lazy.

language barrier is one classic example of this. Many people find ways to live in a foreign country without learning the country's language. And for a while they manage, but there's always a point they reach when they feel completely inadequate, when they need to speak the language and they can't. Instead of doing something about it, they rely on others; they're too lazy to learn a new language.

The V-Woman is a hard worker; she doesn't just work hard with her hands, she works hard with her brains too. She's always learning new things, always investing a little more in her own abilities. And she doesn't depend on others to tell her to do so. She works hard willingly. It's not a burden for her to learn a new language, to learn how to cook, or to learn a new skill.

Too many women treat their most basic to-do lists as burdens. The house needs to be cleaned, but she's too tired to do it, so she turns on the TV and tells herself she'll start her cleaning later in the day. Of course whatever show is on distracts her until it's too late to get anything done. Her laundry piles up, but she tells herself she'll do one load at a time, that way she won't have to spend a whole afternoon taking care of it. But we know how long a shirt takes to be ironed in

the morning when we're usually late. Her clothes get tighter and tighter, but she doesn't want to start a diet, she doesn't want to exercise, she's waiting to get in the mood to lose weight until she's so overweight that the effort to lose the excess is just too much.

The minute something becomes a burden for us, we know we'll not give it our best, so we drag ourselves along. And then we start blaming others for our laziness: "Nobody helps me around the house!" or "I have a life too, you know, I can't be doing laundry all day!" or "I don't know why I'm gaining weight!"

We know when we're working hard and when we're not.

If we work willingly, even when it's heavy work, we show that we can be trusted with more, with better work, with more money, with more people, with better responsibilities. If we don't, we also show that we can't really handle more than what we have now, and perhaps not even that!

Laziness is a feeling and, if you have the habit of living by however you feel, you have a problem. You may want to work hard at something but you may not feel like doing it and, if your heart is often the one that calls the shots, you'd rather be lazy.

If you listen to your heart, you make decisions based on how you feel. Your feelings are here today and gone tomorrow, but consequences are here to stay. How many people are sick today because they didn't feel like eating a healthy diet most of their life? How many women lose their marriage because they didn't take care of it when it needed the most?

It's easy to just sit back and criticize the V-Woman... she's too good to be true. But think about it, can't we all be hard-working? What's stopping us? God doesn't expect us to give what we can't, but what we can, and if we won't give at least what we can, who's to blame for that?

THE PROCRASTINATOR

Another common enemy that stops you from working hard is the spirit of procrastination. Yes, I

> Laziness is a feeling and, if you have the habit of living by however you feel, you have a problem.

think it's a spirit. It's a negative energy that makes everything look like you're in slow motion: you take too long to start something, to finish something, to learn something, to speak to someone about something… everything is always left for later.

Later has no deadlines; later just gives you that extra comfort zone. You feel better because you tell yourself you'll do it later, but at the same time, you don't feel the pressure of a deadline – it's an open deadline. Get it done when you feel like it… that's how things take years to finish!

People know they need to change their life, but they give themselves that later card. Whenever they feel like changing, they pull out that card, as if life can be put on hold to happen on their own terms.

If you let this spirit of procrastination take the driver's seat, you'll never ever get anywhere. You haven't actually learned how to use your time efficiently and, for that reason, your life is always chaotic; things are often left undone.

God doesn't expect us to give what we can't, but what we can…

Some wake up late in the morning, take too long to find an outfit, forget their earrings, leave home without any breakfast, and don't even mention that messy room they leave behind... For some, this happens rarely. For others, it's routine. They look at other women who seem to always have it together and they wonder, what's their secret?

I have their secret and I am giving it away! Here it is! They don't wake up late and they work hard to get things done on time.

Twenty-four hours is enough for anybody to work, eat, rest, get in touch with people and, most importantly, connect with God. But why is it so hard to find people who actually think this way? Why is it that 24 hours a day, 7 days a week, and an average of 30 days a month, and 365 days a year, is just not enough for most people?

When you read about God and everything He has done, you notice exactly the opposite. Everything happened, happens, and will happen as He planned out. Time doesn't put Him down – He controls time. It's godly when we make time for everything; it's godly when we fulfill our plans. Just think of the feeling of fulfillment when you make it happen!

The woman

Delaying your life means low self-esteem, insecurity, irresponsibility, laziness, weakness, doubts, confusion, depression, disorganization, and consequently being UNGODLY.

When you let yourself go and let time escape you, notice how far you feel from God. You're in an endless cycle, you never change, you never become better, you never move on, you're just stuck…

How do you change that?

Do what God does: control your time, have discipline, and never ever let anything delay you again — whether it's laziness, slowness, or distractions. In other words, work hard.

I think I can summarize working hard this way: When you don't do what you feel like, but you do what you have to, you work hard. And that's what this V-Woman does. She willingly works with her hands.

ALONE AND A FOREIGNER

Ruth became a widow at quite a young age. Ever since she married an Israelite, all she could think about was an Israelite's way of life. It was as if she had married Israel too, which by the way, is the ideal way

of handling marriage. This is why you should marry someone you're ready to follow all your life. If you're a Christian and you marry a non-Christian, you might as well say goodbye to your faith. Marriage is about becoming one with another person, which makes it sacred and so important. If you become one with someone who doesn't have the same goals, you'll probably lose your own.

Ruth's mother-in-law Naomi used to tell her tons of stories about Israel, making it impossible for Ruth's heart not to be touched.

So when Ruth's husband died, she couldn't see herself going back to her family, her past, or her gods. And that's when Ruth's story begins. Naomi lost her husband and her two sons, having nothing left but a past. She had no option but to go back to her hometown in Bethlehem and find a way to survive her last years as a poor widow. It's interesting to notice how Naomi's faith quickly grew cold the minute she needed it the most.

> Do what God does: control your time, have discipline...

The woman

> *"It grieves me very much for your sakes that the hand of the LORD has gone out against me!"*

(Ruth 1:13)

To which Ruth replied in verses 16 and 17:

> *Entreat me not to leave you, or to turn back from following after you; for wherever you go, I will go; and wherever you lodge, I will lodge; your people shall be my people, and your God, my God. Where you die, I will die, and there will I be buried. The LORD do so to me, and more also, if anything but death parts you and me.*

Quite a different approach to their shared tragedy! With all those negative vibes from Naomi, Ruth still didn't lose her own faith. She insisted on following Naomi to a strange land and an obscure future. Naomi was a widow, old, poor, and now faithless! It would all depend on Ruth from now on.

Marriage is about becoming one with another person...

As soon as they arrived in Bethlehem, Ruth acquired a whole new position. She was now the breadwinner and, instead of waiting around for a man to show up and marry her, she rolled up her sleeves and began to work like never before.

> *So Ruth the Moabitess said to Naomi,*
> *"Please let me go to the field, and glean*
> *heads of grain after him in whose sight I*
> *may find favor." And she said to her, "Go,*
> *my daughter." Then she left, and went and*
> *gleaned in the field after the reapers.*

(Ruth 2:2,3)

Hard-working people take the initiative. They don't like to wait; they like to make things happen. While Naomi was complaining to the people of her town, "I went out full, and the LORD has brought me home again empty" (Ruth 1:21), Ruth was finding a way to get them out of that miserable situation.

So it was through Ruth's determination to provide stability for herself and her mother-in-law that people began to admire her — rather than Naomi! Naomi, the "woman of faith", was now known as the bitter widow, whereas Ruth, the Moabite foreigner, was now known as the compassionate and hard-working woman of faith.

The woman

Ruth was so different from the other women that the whole town noticed her, including her future husband.

Women tend to forget about what really makes them admirable. They invest so much on their outward looks when, in reality, there will always be more beautiful women out there. Men are not impressed by beauty alone – there's tons of it around to gawk at. Men admire women who are confident enough about themselves and their abilities to do more.

We love to demand attention. I think we're experts at it. But how do we attract the right kind of attention? Not by using the same old methods of everyone else around us: mere appearances. We achieve it by doing what no one else is doing.

Ruth didn't mean to get all that attention. All she wanted was to get things done, to make her mother-in-law stop regretting life, to make up for the lack of a husband and financial support. She worked hard because she knew she had no other choice.

When you work hard, you do what you have to do. Now consider the opposite…

The beauty of this is that the less you have, the more you have. Ruth didn't have anyone to count on,

basically no one to rely on, so she depended on herself. Again, another given trait of hard-working people: they depend on themselves.

When you depend on yourself, you don't wait for anyone, you don't give yourself the luxury of waking up late, wasting or killing time. You do what you have to do because if you don't, nobody else will.

In those days, widows were practically beggars. If they didn't have a husband and children to take care of them, nobody would. Naomi complained about it, Ruth did something about it.

She worked hard under the sun, and inevitably everyone started talking about her. "That's Naomi's daughter-in-law!"

And just as it often happens when people start noticing others who will do what they won't, tongues start to wag. Some admire, others gossip. Soon, the news reached Boaz, the owner of one of the fields where Ruth worked (she gleaned the remainder of

Women tend to forget about what really makes them admirable.

his harvest). Boaz coincidently was related to Naomi, and when he heard about what Ruth was doing, he quickly found a way to meet her.

He gave orders to his field employees to help her by leaving behind some of the stalks of grain they were supposed to reap, so she'd be able to reap them instead.

He also ordered them to respect and treat her well… the man was obviously already enchanted by Ruth.

When you work hard, not only towards your goals, but also for the sake of your own reputation, always overriding your emotions to make the right choices, people can't help but notice you.

Hard-working women deserve happy endings, no matter how unhappy their beginnings were. Ruth soon became Boaz's wife and King David's grandmother. Yes, that's right — a foreigner who worked so hard to keep and live out her new-found faith.

When you work hard, not only towards your goals... people can't help but notice you...

The V-Woman is hard-working, no matter the circumstances, and she works hard willingly. Nobody told Ruth to go to the fields and work hard under the sun – she did that willingly.

What should you be working hard on right now?

What's stopping you?

What can you start doing about it from now on?

Write out a personal plan and stick to it for a week, then two. And when it becomes second nature, write out another one to keep improving on it.

The V woman

My Notes

She finds a way

She is like the merchant ships, she brings her food from afar.

(Proverbs 31:14)

The Proverbs 31 V-Woman lived in a time when there were no supermarkets, no washing machines, no transportation, and no shops. We may wonder how she managed to do everything she did with so few resources. But just like we lived many years without cell phones and still managed to survive, she did alright.

We learn how to live with what we have. That's a beautiful thing about life. All animals learn how to live in their natural habitat. But when that habitat is endangered, life is also endangered... Well, not for the V-Woman.

In this passage, it's clear to me that her hometown wasn't giving her all that she

needed; otherwise, she wouldn't have had to travel far for food – one of life's most basic needs.

She had a family to take care of and she had to find a way to do it.

People often waste time complaining about the things they don't have instead of finding ways to get them. I've lost count how often I've heard... "I don't have a husband and I'm getting old, I feel so lonely..." or "I'm unemployed, that's why I can't afford anything..."

Don't have a husband yet? Work on your relationship with God, make Him your Husband and you'll take care of the loneliness and the age problems all at once. Plus you'll be investing in the One who can find you a partner for life.

> People often waste time complaining about the things they don't have instead of finding ways to get them.

Don't have a job yet? Start doing something to raise money. A friend of mine needed $1,000 in two weeks and so she bought

a few boxes of chocolates, went door-to-door in a nice neighborhood, and earned it by selling them 2 hours a day, 5 days a week.

Most of us love a comfy zone, a place we feel at home, with no worries, no cares, just a sweater and slippers. We let life dictate where we go and so we hardly go anywhere. The V-Woman dictates where she's going. She always finds a way to get there.

WHEN WE'RE UNABLE, HE MAKES US ABLE

I got married when I was 17 years old. Most of the people I knew, except for my own immediate family (surprising, isn't it?), thought I was too young and too immature for such a lifelong commitment. Perhaps I was too young and immature, but there was an ingredient in the mix that wouldn't allow that to become a problem. I had an active faith and a close relationship with God. That's one thing that can never go wrong.

Nevertheless, I was still very inexperienced and quite insecure about myself. God had to take me through a number of different situations in order to mold me into the person I am today (who is still being molded as I write this, to be the person I'll become tomorrow).

I'm not good with memories, but there are some that are engraved in my heart. One of them was this great desire I had to make a difference in the world. I didn't know how – in fact, I had nothing except my faith to help me achieve that. I was a very shy young woman, the kind that would blush if more than one person would look at me at the same time. I couldn't speak in public; I'd swallow my own words and look like a fool every time I tried.

So there I was, with this great desire in my heart and this great impediment in me. I prayed about it. You know when you pray, but know that you're actually making a dumb prayer? I'd pray that God would use me, but then I'd refuse to open my mouth to speak to anyone!

I soon realized that I was not helping God at all and that I'd have to find a way to let Him use me. He said "I am the LORD your God, who brought you out of the land of Egypt; open your mouth wide, and I will fill it" (Psalm 81:10).

In other words, I know where you're coming from, I know you're not capable, but if you'll only open your mouth, I'll give you the abilities you lack.

And with that word I began opening my mouth. I'd blush, I'd have tears in my eyes, I'd be laughed at and

ridiculed in front of others (on a separate note, I think it's so uncalled for when people laugh at other people's weaknesses). It was not easy, and I had to go against the shy person I had been up until then.

When everything around you tells you "no", that's when you have to find a way. It's easy to find a way when everything is working in your favor. In fact, you're not finding a way at all; you're just going with the flow. But we all know that life's flow hardly ever goes in the right direction… we need to create our own current, we need to find another way, dig a way out of our own personal prisons.

How many women are so independent in their careers and finances, but imprisoned by their own emotional struggles? What's the use of all the money or high status? Anything that binds you should be seen as an opportunity to find a way out.

Eventually, as I kept on speaking in public, and still blushing every now and then, I got used to it and God found a way to answer my prayer.

> When everything around you tells you "no", that's when you have to find a way.

First I found a way, and then He found a way. Every miracle and answered prayer begins with us.

ABUSED AND DESPISED

Tamar was one of these women, though the Bible doesn't give many details about her aside from one chapter in the Bible, Genesis 38. She was given into marriage to a man named Er, one of Judah's sons. In those times, women rarely had the option of choosing their own husbands, and Tamar was unfortunate to marry a very evil man. Er was so evil that God had to take his life at a young age (the Bible actually says that!), leaving Tamar a young childless widow.

In those days, widows were seen as burdens. However, if they had brothers-in-law, they still had hope of being taken care of. The tradition was that the next oldest brother should marry his brother's widow, have a child with her

First I found a way, and then He found a way. Every miracle and answered prayer begins with us.

so that his dead brother would have a descendent here on earth.

Onan, Er's brother, was obligated to marry Tamar and take care of her as a husband. And if she became pregnant, the child would belong to Er's descendants. Onan was as evil as his brother and didn't want to give his brother an heir, but still liked the idea of sleeping with his widow Tamar, and made sure he didn't impregnate her on purpose.

Onan didn't love her, just like Er didn't. She felt used once again, and worst of all, used by men who were supposed to have faith in God. Onan died young too. God saw Tamar's situation as He does any woman who's taken advantage of. Whenever you're in a vulnerable situation, understand this – rather, hold on to this forever: you have God to champion your cause.

> *The LORD is near to those who have a broken heart, and saves such as have a contrite spirit.*

> (Psalm 34:18)

The only remaining brother to Er was Shelah, Judah's youngest son. Obviously, by this time, people began to blame Tamar for the two coincidental deaths.

The V woman

Often, people rarely look at the facts, they only jump to conclusions. Tamar was now known as the black widow of the town – marry her and you'll surely die!

Judah, afraid of losing his only remaining son Shelah, gave her the excuse that Shelah was still too young to marry, and that she could wait for him to come of age back in her father's house... poor woman, deceived by both husbands and now her father-in-law too.

But as any V-Woman, Tamar didn't give up. In fact, she didn't live grudgingly either. I'm sure all her family felt disgusted with the way Judah and his family treated her. She was an outcast; humiliated and deceived by those who were supposed to care for her.

But instead of crying day and night about how unfair her life had been, Tamar found a way to get what was rightfully hers – her own family.

Much later, after Judah's wife had died, Tamar took courage and began to figure out a plan for her own future.

She learned that Judah was going on a journey and would take his usual traveling route. She took off her widow's clothes, disguised herself as a prostitute, and waited for Judah to pass by along the road. She probably didn't tell anyone, because if she had, she'd be stoned to death. Who would understand her? At this point, only God really. Every time we need to do something drastic to find a way out of our situation, God understands. He knew that she wasn't really being a prostitute, but she was using that disguise to get what was due to her: a descendant of Judah's bloodline (Israel's blood).

Judah fell right into her trap, and as payment for her services, he gave her his seal and cord, and his staff, pledging to pay her back as soon as he got home. He honored his word by sending payment later, but she wasn't there anymore, she was gone.

Three months later, the news of Tamar's pregnancy shocked everyone and, when Judah heard of it, he ordered her brought out and burned to death for her crime against his sons and his family (as if they had been good to her!). Oh how irritating it is to see people being so self-righteous about some things,

> Often, people rarely look at the facts, they only jump to conclusions.

and so casual about others. Either we're righteous or we're not. He slept with a prostitute three months earlier, and that was perfectly okay with him. But his daughter-in-law, who had the right to bear him an heir, showed up pregnant and all of a sudden she's the devil! How typical of religious people.

Thankfully, God had given Tamar wisdom to cover herself. She quickly showed him the seal and cord, and the staff he had given her as a pledge of payment, which certainly humbled him. She gave birth to twins who belonged to the Lord Jesus' lineage alongside other great men and women of faith – quite a turnaround for a rejected widow!

Tamar's attitude was not seen as fornication or 'sleeping around' or having a child out of wedlock. This was a very important feature of Jewish culture, a right guarded by a God-appointed law.

Every time we need to do something drastic to find a way out of our situation, God understands.

So Judah acknowledged them and said, "She has been

more righteous than I, because I did not give her to Shelah my son." And he never knew her again.

(Genesis 38:26)

Judah was humbled by Tamar's wise attitude.

What would most women do in her place? Take off the widow's clothes a long time ago and carry on with all that hurt from the past, venting her frustrations on the next relationship, just like many women who keep raising that all-men-are-the-same flag. Where does it take them? What does that do to them? If anything, the inability to find a good relationship!

Another beautiful trait Tamar had was that she remained faithful to Judah's family, even though they certainly did not deserve it. Perhaps she was being faithful to God instead; it's so much easier to do things for God than for men, because He always honors us and He never owes us anything.

Many wives of unbelievers have changed their husbands into men of faith because of this attitude. Some started submitting to their drunken and addicted husbands as if they were doing it for God, and their attitudes showed so much love that their husbands actually had remorse for the treatment they were giving them in return, and changed.

What problem have you been stuck in?

Think of ways to get rid of it and whatever you decide to do, do it consistently. One-time deals usually do not work.

My Notes

She's disciplined

She also rises while it is yet night, and provides food for her household, and a portion for her maidservants.

(Proverbs 31:15)

I t's not easy to rise while it's still dark outside. You feel like you're not supposed to be up, that you're fighting against common sense when the pillow hugs you so perfectly, the mattress comfortably conforms to your body, and the duvet is keeping you so warm… but it's 6am and you know that if you're not up soon, you won't have everything ready in time. Never mind the chilly room, never mind that your body doesn't want to start the day – your head does.

The V-Woman is disciplined. She knows that if she doesn't organize her time properly, things will be left undone. That's why she wakes up early and doesn't waste time

on temporary "good" feelings. Her body doesn't dictate her day – her mind does.

The Proverbs 31 V-Woman also had maids and could have given herself the luxury of sleeping till late... But it's interesting that, even though she had people to provide the food for her household, she took that responsibility upon herself. It was her duty, her own concern, and in order for it to come out well, she had to do it herself. She not only prepared food for her own family, she did it for her maids too. What an amazing woman!

I'm sure she kept thinking, "If you want something done well, do it yourself." Things are never done exactly the way you want them when delegated to others. That's just a fact. But you know that you can't do everything you want all by yourself – that's also a fact. And this is where discipline comes in.

> Things are never done exactly the way you want them when delegated to others.

What is discipline but a way of handling life in a more organized way?

Remember how things were in school. We had

one principal, a principal's office, teachers, a teachers' lounge, classrooms, a gym, a cafeteria and a playground. We also had a bell that rang to let us know the time for the next class or break. The whole system worked to instill discipline from the time we were children. We feared the principal and avoided being sent to his office. We had to see the teachers' lounge as out of bounds, and stick to playing or hanging around in our own playground. We ate in the cafeteria, not in the classrooms or in the gym because those were meant to be used for classes. We listened to the teachers because of the position they had.

That's how discipline works. Everything is in place for a reason. The V-Woman had maids to do the things she could not do, and yet, she was still the one calling the shots at home, unlike so many mothers these days who leave their children to be raised by a babysitter. I totally agree with the need for babysitters… but to raise your children? That's not right.

You don't have to be home all day long to raise a child, but the little time you are home should be enough to give him or her love, care, understanding, important life lessons, and all that comes with a good upbringing.

When a woman is disciplined, she knows what's important in her life. Nothing comes before her priorities.

I remember a mother who came to me in tears because of a regret she'd been carrying for years. It was now too late to make things work. Her children were all grown up and hated her for the frustrations she had poured out on them the few hours a day she spent at home while they were young. At the time, she thought she was doing them a favor by working hard as a single mother, but in the process she was actually pushing them away. For a time, she looked for a man to give them some kind of stability at home, but those various relationships just made her children grow even wearier of her.

Discipline was all she needed. She could have worked hard and been disciplined with her time. She could have looked for a partner and still been disciplined about it. She could have rebuked her children and been disciplined with the way she did it.

Discipline can be found everywhere. Look at the animals, nature, and time itself. Why would we not follow this most basic rule of life?

DISCIPLINE IS DYNAMIC

Dynamic women can do many things at once. They're usually the ones we often look at and wonder how they manage to do everything and still look great.

While some of them inherit the multi-tasking gene, others learn this out of necessity. For that reason, they don't waste time on day dreaming, watching TV, browsing the Net, chatting on the phone, texting friends, gossiping over lunch, and even complaining of aches and pains.

Obviously, they do have fun. But there's a time and place for that. They think of better ways to do what they do, to make what they do better, to make a difference. In light of that, they normally don't get into trouble. Their mind is very productive and so it's never idle, never empty to make room for ridiculous ideas or thoughts.

This dynamic V-Woman plans her day and week ahead of time. Everything fits perfectly: her time with God, family, home, work, learning something new, health and beauty. All this control makes her a happy

> Discipline can be found everywhere. Look at the animals, nature, and time itself.

woman, pleasant to be around. Her husband and children admire her. Her friends love being with her. Her co-workers respect her.

But she doesn't always get it right, because she's not Mrs. Perfect, as she's often called. She just doesn't waste time with her failures. She learns from them and moves on. There's no time to cry over them and ponder the whys.

She is fast. She thinks fast, she reacts fast, she starts fast, she walks fast. The faster she is, the closer she gets to her goals that day. The dynamic woman gets things done. She hates to leave things for later. If there's something she needs to do, she'll make time to do it or else, it'll disrupt her sleep. The V-Woman is efficient. Give her a duty, and she'll have it done on time and in a better way than what you were expecting.

She's competitive in some ways. It's not that she wants to be better than others, but there's a drive within her that makes her want to do and be

This dynamic V-Woman plans her day and week ahead of time.

better than she was yesterday. She doesn't need anybody to tell her what to do, this drive is sufficient. She's independent.

Sometimes she'll crash, and it's often because she's so much of a multi-tasker that people tend to depend on her to put out all kinds of fires. In the middle of all these things going on inside and around her, she still needs to look good and be kind...

BUSY AND STRESSED

Mary and Martha were two sisters who had the privilege of receiving the Lord Jesus and His disciples in their home. It wasn't common for the Lord Jesus to do this; He often spent His "spare" time with the disciples, so it was truly an honor to receive Him as their guest.

Martha quickly got going all over the place, as I'd imagine any of us would. Imagine yourself having 13 unexpected guests for dinner? Clean this, cook that, serve this, arrange that... suddenly, as she was passing by the living room where the Lord Jesus was seated, she was struck by the sight of her own sister, Mary, who was supposed to be fixing something instead of sitting down as if there was nothing going on.

"What a nerve!" she must have felt.

Oh yes, Martha got mad. How dare her sister treat her that way? She wasn't going to let it go, and pretend that she hadn't seen it… Oh no, she was going to point it out and she was going to do it in front of the Lord Jesus Himself. That way, He'd appreciate all the work she was doing all by herself and He'd condemn her sister Mary. She deserved it.

> *Lord, do You not care that my sister has left me to serve alone? Therefore tell her to help me.*

> (Luke 10:40)

Did she just demand something from the Lord Jesus? Was He the One at fault here? I'm sure that as soon as Martha spoke those words, she felt terribly bad about it; after all, the problem was Mary, not the Lord Jesus.

But isn't that what happens when there's too much to do and too little time left, and we feel as though we are losing control? It's at such times that we also tend to lose control of our tongue. We say words we don't mean – and usually, words that haunt us for a very long time. Once you say them, they're out; they'll never ever cease to exist.

That's how hurts are born. And let's be honest with ourselves: we women have this terrible talent of putting people down, making them feel as small as a squashed bug. It's the tone we use and the below-the-belt comments we make. And worst of all is that we often don't realize what we are doing.

But the Lord Jesus didn't act as Martha expected. He didn't take her side at all, even though it appeared that she was the only one doing anything for His visit.

> *Martha, Martha, you are worried and troubled about many things. But one thing is needed, and Mary has chosen that good part, which will not be taken away from her.*

(Luke 10:41,42)

And that's what happens to any of us who so often perform our "miracle" of being all over the

We say words we don't mean... words that haunt us for a very long time.

place, getting all kinds of things done at the same time but without discipline – we forget about the important things in life.

Mary knew that a lot was expected from her as one of the hostesses of that important visit, but she decided to take advantage of the presence of that visitor, instead of treating it like a big dinner event in her house. Mary's decision changed her life forever.

This is the key to being organized: to know your priorities. If you're organized but your priorities are out of order, you're still all over the place and missing the key point of why you're being organized in the first place.

There will always be many things to do; there will always be little time to do them. Don't fall into the rut that a lot of women do these days. They're losing their family, their self-respect, their reputation, and even their youth because they won't put what is important first.

...we women have this terrible talent of putting people down, making them feel as small as a squashed bug.

LISTENING TO TOO MANY VOICES

Men are different from us. They are wired to focus and conquer. We strive to do what they do and still be a mother, a wife, and the household queen. But we are not them, and we can't expect to fulfill both a man's and a woman's roles without compromising ourselves.

A man can be a good father while spending only a few hours of the day with his children, knowing that his wife is raising them well. A mother sacrifices precious moments that are lost forever when she chooses a career over her children, and she feels that loss intensely. A man can still be single in his 30s and take his time, but for us, the clock is always ticking. But something tells us that we are being cheated if we don't live men's lives and have their freedom.

This control bug can lead us to make terrible decisions. It's fueled by the pressure that is placed on women practically everywhere we look: our education system, the economy, social expectations, cultural norms, advertising... It's as if everybody out there was targeting us to become what they want us to be.

But the V-Woman knows what comes first. She is disciplined and she knows that without her spiritual life in place, she has nothing, she'll do nothing right,

and she'll never get anywhere. The only way for you to ever be good enough for yourself is to do what Mary did: sit down at the Lord Jesus' feet and listen to what He has to say. He knows exactly what you need and He'll guide you on how to get there.

What's lacking in your spiritual life at this moment? Why?

What will you start doing about that from now on? How?

My Notes

She finds opportunities

*She considers a field and buys it; from
her profits she plants a vineyard.*

(Proverbs 31:16)

The week ahead of you is going to be busy: grocery shopping, appointments, guests, payments, tests, meetings, reports, cleaning, washing, cooking, working, counseling, shopping, reading... You note everything down on a piece of paper, you scratch your head, and those new lines on your forehead start to form...

Sometimes things we do suck out all the time we have, leaving us little time for new things, new ideas, and new opportunities.

Opportunities are like hidden treasures, and not many clean signs point to

them — few of us notice them. But while the V-Woman controls her finances, she's also on the lookout for new opportunities to increase her gain. She could have used her profits to buy new fabric to clothe her family, but she decided to use it on more ways to increase their gain... plant a vineyard. Who would think of that?

People who are always on the lookout for new opportunities look at things from the top — so they see farther. They see things that are not so in-your-face. That's what makes them different; that's what makes them stand out. They do things nobody thought of doing. They always seem to be one step ahead. They take more initiatives.

And when you take more initiative, you're bound to find opportunities. People who complain that they never get better opportunities in life are the same ones who keep on waiting for something to happen. They wait and wait, every single day, every single week, every single month,

> People who are always on the lookout for new opportunities look at things from the top – so they see farther.

every single year. They keep telling themselves "Maybe I'll have better luck next time."

Complacency kills opportunities. While you're alright with the same old thing every day, you miss the point of what life is all about. Life is about changing; it's about getting better, doing better, growing. Life is full of opportunities, no matter where you're from, where you live, who you are, or who you've been. The future depends on us, on what we do today. If we don't do anything different, the future will probably just get worse.

Back in December 2007, my husband was transferred to work in Texas. We were used to a lot of work in London, daily meetings, weekly pastors' meetings, TV and radio programs, group leaders' meetings, and so much more. We felt a bit tied down upon our arrival in Houston when we learned we were to make meetings only three times a week.

Within a month in Houston, we began noticing that there was no active youth group in the Church, but who were we to tell the leadership that? We prayed about it. But as we all know, prayer always returns with a so-what-are-you-going-to-do-about-it response, so we had the courage to ask permission to start working on it.

Beginning a youth group is not easy at all. Our church in Houston hardly had any young people coming, and the few that came would sit in the back of the church and chew gum. We had to dig deep within us to wake up that much needed level of patience that had been lying dormant for some time. Youth meetings were mentally draining, especially because we hardly saw any fruit coming out of it. But we didn't give up: we started getting ideas from other Youth leaders, we started being creative, we started doing things we never thought we'd do; and things began to pick up.

Today the youth group we began has expanded to many other cities in Texas and across America in just over 2 years.

We saw a need and, instead of pointing fingers, we found a solution for it. We found an opportunity, we took the initiative, we sacrificed.

DISQUALIFIED WITH A PAST

Mary Magdalene was delivered from seven demons. The Bible doesn't specifically say what her problems were, but she surely suffered spiritually.

From the day of her deliverance onwards, Mary lived to serve the Lord Jesus. She was eternally grateful; and everywhere her Lord went, there she was after Him, serving Him and His disciples. The woman couldn't get enough of that new faith; it was as if her eyes had finally opened her eyes after being blind all her life.

But her Lord didn't stay on earth very long; everything happened from one day to the next, as she watched Him die the most cursed death in history, hung on a cross. Mary was one of the few of the Lord Jesus' followers who remained by His side during His death.

And as soon as the Sabbath was over, she and some of her friends who felt the same way towards the Lord Jesus quickly made their way to His tomb in order to have one last look at Him. His was one controversial death. There were those who were totally in favor of it and those who were totally against it, but those in favor were more powerful.

We found an opportunity, we took the initiative, we sacrificed.

As it has always been in this world, evil usually takes the lead.

Mary Magdalene was actually risking her life by showing up at the Lord Jesus' tomb. Roman soldiers were supposed to be guarding it, but she went anyway; her reason to live had been taken away from her. She didn't have much to live for anymore, or so she thought. But when she got there, the soldiers were not there. The tomb was open, and only the Lord Jesus' burial cloth was left.

Mary wept bitterly thinking she had taken too long to come and see Him. But an angel came to the rescue and spoke to her and her friends:

> *Do not be afraid, for I know that you seek Jesus who was crucified. He is not here; for He is risen, as He said. Come, see the place where the*

After the greatest sacrifice God had made for humankind, He cared enough to show Himself first to a woman...

Lord lay. And go quickly and tell His disciples that He is risen from the dead, and indeed He is going before you into Galilee; there you will see Him. Behold, I have told you.

(Matthew 28:5-7)

As they believed, "they went out quickly from the tomb with fear and great joy, and ran to bring His disciples word" (Matthew 28:8). Notice that they left quickly – these women were dynamic!

The Lord Jesus didn't wait too long either – He met them on their way and said, "Rejoice!"... After so much love and devotion to Him, even during tough times, He had to show Himself to them first.

This goes against those who think the Bible is male-oriented. After the greatest sacrifice God had made for humankind, He cared enough to show Himself first to a woman, who was no better than anyone else, but who was there.

Mary and her friends didn't wait until things looked peaceful again, they didn't wait for the disciples to tell them what to do, they didn't wait to be called or to hear the latest news. They went to the tomb regard-

less of what people could do to them. That's how opportunities are found.

God meets half-way those who will reach out half-way to Him. They don't need to be perfect; they just need to take the initiative. He often shows opportunities to those who are sensitive to His voice, but it's up to them to take the initiative and do something about that suggestion. They can either listen, find it interesting, and wish someone would do something about it. Or they can listen, find it interesting, and actually do something about it.

Look at how taking a simple initiative changed Mary's life. It gave her a whole new perspective of life, knowing that her Lord was no longer dead but alive and with her.

The V-Woman doesn't complain about lack of opportunities – she finds opportunities. Even the term itself can already give you a hint of how that can be done; you need to look in order to find.

If you keep on waiting for opportunities to knock on your door, you'll never get to meet them. You need to get out and look for them – only then you will find them.

What have you been waiting for to happen in your life?

What initiatives can you start taking today on that will stop the waiting and start the process of achieving?

God meets half-way those who will reach out half-way to Him. They don't need to be perfect; they just need to take the initiative.

My Notes

She's strong

She girds herself with strength, and strengthens her arms

(Proverbs 31:17)

The exercises I struggle with the most when I go to the gym are the ones that demand strength from my arms. For those I tend to choose the lightest weights, which still make my arms shake every time. This V-Woman was definitely stronger than me, carrying all her goods from afar; you can imagine how fit she was. But that's not the strength the Bible is referring to here; otherwise, some of us would have to spend the rest of our lives in a gym!

Physical strength has its benefits, but it's not a real need for most of us (especially those who have strong men at home, like a husband and a son – thank

you guys for always helping me out!). Spiritual strength, however, is a need we all have — no matter if we are physically weak or strong. When life slaps us in the face, our physical strength is worthless if we're not fit spiritually.

A strong woman will keep on moving even when everyone around her has pressed the "pause" button. A strong woman does not give up. The V-Woman above knew about this and so she girded herself with the strength she would need: her faith.

According to the Longman Dictionary of Contemporary English, "if you gird for something, or gird yourself for something, especially something difficult, you prepare for it."

Now that's something few people do. People are always working on their appearance, their career, their finances, their lifestyle, their social networks, their relation-

> When life slaps
> us in the face,
> our physical strength
> is worthless if
> we're not
> fit spiritually.

ships... but what about their spirit? Who's strengthening that? Who's preparing for that?

At 3 years of age, my son loved it when his daddy placed him on the top of a high cabinet so he'd safely jump into his daddy's arms. After each time, he'd say the same thing: "Do it again Daddy!" This is one of the most amazing traits found in children – they believe. They don't think of the possibility that Daddy could easily drop them or miss... it doesn't even cross their mind.

My son believed in his daddy so much that he put all his fears behind to just jump into his arms. He believed, which made him brave enough to jump.

One of the easiest things you can choose to do is to believe; and you'd be surprised at how much belief is related to strength.

When you don't believe in yourself, it's almost certain that you will fail in everything you do. You know that. Everybody knows that. 'Believe in yourself' is one of the most common sayings out there. But practicing it is one of the rarest. And the most common reason why a woman doesn't believe in herself is simple: she's weak-minded.

A weak-minded woman will take in any evil thought that is blown into her mind. She's not the only

one who gets them, but she's the kind of woman that accepts them. Everyone hears evil thoughts from time to time, at least once a day (on a good day that is), but you don't have to open the doors of your mind to them. You don't have to consider them; you don't even have to notice that they're there. You're welcome to shut the door in their face. In fact, if you want to protect yourself and your family, this is exactly what you must do every time they knock on your door.

The more you do it, the more you get used to it, and the more you start respecting yourself for keeping a positive attitude about yourself and your life. And that right there is how you develop your strength.

But that's just 50% of the strength you need — and it's a shame to see how many people just rely on that 50%. They believe in themselves, they conquer the world, but they lack the other 50% of the strength to overcome life's sudden accidents and misfortunes, such as diseases, break-ups, unfaithfulness, disappointments, bankruptcy, disasters, and so many other occurrences that are beyond their power. The other 50% is, of course, to believe in God. It's to know that His arms will always be there to catch you — whether you jump, get pushed, or fall.

The V-Woman had the whole package. She had her own strength and God's too. Faith in God is the most efficient way to live a full, happy life. You'll never find a fulfilled person who doesn't also have an active faith in God. You can find the rich and the famous without this particular strength, and that's why they'll always lack something in their lives to feel totally complete. It's sad to know that their smile is just a façade, a pretense of how fulfilled they wished they were.

This attitude of pretending to be stronger than we are usually starts around our teenage years. It's interesting how many parents often neglect those years in their children's lives because they also felt neglected. But it really is a façade if you think about it. As teenagers, we begin to understand how life works. It's the age when we start making sense of our feelings and what's happening around us. Since the discovery of the adult world is all so new and strange, many times we don't know how to behave.

We become too afraid to show others what's go-

Faith in God is the most efficient way to live a full, happy life.

ing on, and that's when we decide to put on a mask. At home, we don't communicate, because if we speak too much and spend a little more time with our parents, they'll find out what's going on inside our heads – and then it'll be so boring to hear them lecture us about things they hardly understand themselves.

In school, however, we're anxious to fit in, and since people don't know us as well as at home, we fake everything about us. We pretend not to care about things that we do care about, we pretend we like things that we don't, we do things we don't want to do, and we talk about things we don't have a clue about.

Now imagine everybody doing that at the same time. No wonder teenagers are undervalued. Adults misunderstand them completely. And teens are often just a step away from doing the exact opposite of what their adult role models advise.

> An active faith is not the kind of faith we often see around us. It's not about being religious... An active faith is a real relationship with God.

They want to try out the world, make their own mistakes, and learn to live life their way. That little snowball soon becomes an avalanche.

These young women believe in themselves enough to let go of their families, to live independently, and to throw themselves into an uncertain future. But their strength is based on their own small being, prone to so many mistakes and wrong decisions. Life will often not turn out as they expected and many of them end up living the same old life as their parents. And so the cycle continues. They grow up and try to give their children the same advice that their parents tried to give them when they were growing up, but their children behave just as they did... life continues in a never-ending sad, sad story.

Had an active faith been included somewhere along the way, things would have turned out differently. Their strength would have been enough and they would have avoided that cycle of disaster. An active faith is not the kind of faith we often see around us. It's not about being religious or going to church every week. An active faith is a real relationship with God. You know Him, you speak to Him, you listen to Him, you do His will, you live according to His wishes, you serve Him.

The woman

You can't really have a relationship with God without giving up a lot of who you are and what you want. I'll tell you how it happened to me in particular.

FAITH IS PERSONAL

Nobody really thought much of me when I was growing up, and looking back, I can understand why. I would often hide in my younger sister's shadow. She was the funny one, the bold one, the strong one, the interesting one, and the more popular one. I didn't have a problem with that. As a matter of fact, I enjoyed all the attention she got; it made me feel less guilty that I didn't have to go through what she did with her birth defect – she was born with a cleft palate.

In my lonely little shell I began clinging on to God; and at first, it was mostly out of fear. I was afraid of going to hell[1] . I'd often hear about it in church and it scared me. I used to pray "God forgive me" about 100 times a day, just to make sure I was still saved. I had nightmares almost every night, but that wasn't the worst of it…

[1] Everlasting punishment after death for living a sinful life away from God (Isaiah 66:24; Matthew 10:28; 24:46; Revelation 20:12,15).

I started sleep walking. I'd go to sleep in my bed and wake up the next day in some other room of the house. I once did that while we had guests and when I woke up I found myself sleeping in their room. It was one of the most embarrassing moments of my life!

I was baptized in water, but still, things didn't change... No matter how much I read the Bible, how much I asked God to forgive me, I still didn't have the faith that my parents had. I remember hearing message upon message and not understanding anything. It was as if nothing in church ever spoke to me.

I began imitating my mother in prayer. Lifting my hands and even speaking in tongues, just like she did. And still... nothing.

Meanwhile, things started to get worse. I started having all kinds of evil thoughts, the kind I even feel ashamed to write about. I didn't understand it though. How could I, someone who didn't do

> You can't really have a relationship with God without giving up a lot of who you are and what you want.

anything bad (so I thought), who lived a sheltered life, who practically grew up indoors playing on carpet my whole childhood, possibly have so many hidden evil struggles?

Nobody knew what was going on. Sometimes I'd feel this huge hole in my chest, and it hurt. It was a pain I could not pinpoint. "Why am I here?", "Why do I exist?", and "Is God really real?" were just some of the tormenting questions that I'd have. And on top of it, I suffered from asthma. When it hit, which happened about every other day, I'd have to sit and stay in one place the whole day. I couldn't speak to anyone, I couldn't do anything. The worst time was at night when I had to make myself sleep sitting down, wheezing and gasping for breath, sounding like a bunch of cats were whirring inside of me. I lost count how many times I was rushed to the hospital.

...things started to get worse.
I started having all kinds of evil thoughts...

Still I kept reading my Bible, going to church, and making my fear-driven prayers.

I had a perfect family but I didn't have a perfect life. My parents had the strength I didn't have. It helped me sometimes but, at the end of the day, you know how it is. Life is personal, and so is faith. Everybody around you can have an active faith and they may help you take on a positive attitude, but they can't give you what you need to keep it up for long. You need to have it for yourself.

I was 16 when the spiritual penny finally dropped. I remember going to church that day, as I had done all my life. There was nothing special about that Sunday, but for some reason, the message spoken from the altar came at me head-on. I felt convicted, lost, the sinner I didn't know I was.

When the altar-call came to acknowledge how lost I was before God, I didn't care about the thoughts that shouted "What are the people in the church going to say if they see you go up front? Just pray in your seat; nobody needs to know your spiritual condition!" and "But you speak in tongues! You're baptized; of course you're converted, aren't you?

I got up and went straight forward. I didn't look to either side; I didn't care about what people thought of me then. All I cared about was the fact that I needed a Savior urgently.

I poured myself out before God that day. I had never spoken to Him so sincerely, so open-heartedly, so deeply. At one point I stopped speaking and would just sob, my words didn't come out right; my cry was too intense. I gave all of myself to God, all my fears, my doubts, my plans, my worries, my thoughts, and my future. And in return, He gave me the new birth[2].

That was the day I met God for myself; no more doubts, no more weird evil thoughts, no more sleep walking, no more void in my heart, no more panic attacks. I was happy as I had never been before… my life literally changed that day.

Everything around me was still the same. My family was still there, happy as always. My friends and my church, still a joy in my life. But now I was different, I liked being me, for the first time in my life, I was happy being me.

The strength I received that day is the strength that you need in order to be a V-Woman. Everyone goes through hardships in life, everyone gets disappointed now and then, but not everyone has the strength they

---

[2] When you give your whole life to God and He in turn, performs the miracle of the new birth in you, so that you become a true child of God (John 3:3; 2 Corinthians 5:17; 1 Peter 3-4).

need to keep going when these things happen. Most people stay stuck in that period of never-ending depression, numbed by medication and psychotherapy. They gain some satisfaction that someone else in the world cares about their sorrows, for an hour a week at an extravagant cost.

UNPOPULAR AND RIDICULED

Noah's wife spent about one hundred years of her life hearing her husband say that the world was going to end. She saw his struggle to convince everyone around him that they needed to turn back to God but nobody listened. She helped her husband build an ark that in everybody's eyes looked like a crazy circus act. She had many opportunities to doubt her husband, to lose faith in what God had told him, and to stop supporting him.

Everyone goes through hardships in life, everyone gets disappointed now and then, but not everyone has the strength they need to keep going...

The woman

But she was strong. So strong that she raised her children in that evil environment and still managed to keep them in the same faith. She was alone. None of her neighbors or relatives believed. She was going to have to see them all perish in the flood.

Noah's wife was in the background of Noah's story. You won't read much about her in the Bible, but you can tell that God needed a strong woman by Noah's side to endure all the persecution and difficulties he'd have to face while carrying out God's plan.

Just like today, whenever you try to show people the truth, they ignore you, they hate you for it, they make up stories about you. It's easier to just not say anything, to spare ourselves that extra burden, but that's not what God called us to do.

We're all supposed to be His witnesses in this dying world, and if we don't do what we're supposed to do, we don't deserve to get in the ark either.

The V-Woman is strong, and because of her strength, she touches peoples' lives.

The V-Woman is strong, and because of

her strength, she touches peoples' lives. Her strength is so much more than what you can see outwardly. It's a deep-rooted strength and nothing and no one can put her down.

Have you cultivated this inner strength lately?

What do you have to do in order to achieve it? How?

The V woman

My Notes

She appreciates

She perceives that her merchandise is good,
and her lamp does not go out by night.

(Proverbs 31:18)

Many women want to have a family of their own, a husband to belong to, a child to raise, and a home to care for. But it's funny how many of these will completely forget what they said they wanted the minute they get these things…

"I'm too tired to cook dinner every night. Here, serve yourself this frozen microwave dinner I bought the other day."

"Who do you think you are to tell me what I should or shouldn't do? I may be your wife but I have a life too!"

"I can't wait for my child to go off to school and give me a break!"

"I don't have time to care for this house; my family had better accept it."

These and other more shameful comments are made every single day by women who one day wished they could have it all, and now that "all" has become a burden for them.

The V-Woman appreciates what she has. And the way she shows it is by providing her children, husband, and home with the best. It's the way she joyfully cooks, cleans, irons, does her groceries, stocks them, organizes, decorates, and invests. Such basic housewife responsibilities reveal how much you appreciate your family.

I've heard of wives "saving money" on food in order to buy themselves a new dress… husbands having to iron their own shirts in the morning because there were none in the closet for them to wear… children being raised by TV, Internet, and video games for the lack of anything else to do when they're home from school. It's a sad picture.

...basic housewife responsibilities reveal how much you appreciate your family.

Worst of all, if she can't even appreciate those she sees, how can she ever appreciate God?

WHERE APPRECIATION BEGINS

You can only start appreciating something when you understand its meaning and know its value. Let's talk about you for a while. If you can't appreciate yourself, you will have a much harder time appreciating those around you. Perhaps that's why you know you have to do more for your family but you feel you can't, you have nothing left to spare.

It's really about how little you've thought of yourself all this time. There's always at least one thing about you that you hate. And once you hate something about yourself, you begin a chain reaction, hating everything else about yourself because you assume you're just not good enough anyway.

You look around the house and you're convinced you could never be a good homemaker; and so, instead of wasting your time trying, you just decide to let others think that's just the way you are. You feel the need to convince yourself that you're not the domestic type and so you slack off, without even realizing that you're fulfilling a self-prophecy.

The woman

You see yourself that way, so of course others begin seeing the same thing; it's like another verse in Proverbs: "For as he thinks in his heart, so is he" (Proverbs 23:7).

We determine who we are by the way we think of ourselves. The V-Woman perceived that her merchandise was good. She worked hard for it, why not recognize all the effort she put into it? Now let's go back to you.

FEARFULLY AND WONDERFULLY MADE

You began to exist on the day that your parents came together. Let's start appreciating you from way back then…

In the beginning, you already showed your potential to become somebody because out of the millions of other sperm cells swimming towards the egg at top speed, you were the one that made it through.

Then the time you spent in your mother's womb may have offered more challenges. Who knows? There may have been health or emotional issues that your mother was going through that inevitably had an impact on you. It wasn't your fault, but you were part of her and so you were also exposed to what she was exposed to.

But you made it through. You were born and you made it till here with nothing but information. Yes, that's right! You have been taught a lot through the years, in school, in relationships, at home, facing problems, interacting with people -- and so you got yourself to who and where you are today. If you like where you are, great! If you don't, you still need to appreciate the fact that you haven't given up on yourself like so many have.

Perhaps all your life you've learned to accept things as they come along. If you're poor, that's what life reserved for you, just live with it. If you're a loner, that's what you deserve for doing all the things you did or didn't do. But what if you changed that state of mind? What if you started walking down another path, the mysterious one you've always thought was out of your league? What if you decided today to be the woman you were meant to be, instead of the woman you are today?

Deep within you, there's a winner someone who's just waiting for a chance to prove you wrong. This win-

We determine who we are by the way we think of ourselves.

The woman

ner needs to get out and do the things you've been afraid of, do the things you don't believe you can, or should.

You'll be surprised at how much you can change just by beginning to appreciate these little things about yourself. Recognize that your ability is beyond your understanding. Stop trying to make sense of it, go ahead and start the process of using it.

Once you begin to appreciate yourself, you'll start appreciating others around you too. And your behavior will clearly show it, since it won't be because you have to, but because you want to.

Do you know what happens when you begin appreciating others? They start appreciating you back.

Deep within you, there's a winner someone who's just waiting for a chance to prove you wrong.

ORPHAN AND DISCRIMINATED

Esther was a young, single, innocent, Jewish orphan girl when King

Ahasuerus decided to round up all the beautiful young virgins from his vast 27 provinces (a kingdom that spanned from India to Ethiopia) in order to select a new queen. He didn't really ask who wanted to become a candidate, he just took all the young women from their home who possessed the qualities he needed for a queen and forced them to live in the palace for a period of 12 months' preparation. Once they were prepared, he'd sleep with them, and decide who would be his queen. Those who were not chosen would, from then on, become his concubines.

This idea came about because of King Ahasuerus' disappointment of Queen Vashti, who lacked appreciation for him. The man was harsh. He wasn't a man who feared God and he had a lot of power. You can imagine what that could do to anybody.

Jews at the time were not appreciated at all; in fact, they were persecuted (as usual) by most nations. Israel, being the first nation through which God chose to show Himself to the world has always been more hated than appreciated.

As you can imagine, Esther wasn't exactly the most appreciated of the candidates, and yet, she was different. Esther didn't have much compared to the other young

The woman

ladies in the king's courts. She was different from most of them; it wasn't only because she was a Jew (which was kept a secret under her uncle's advice) or because she was an orphan. Her difference was within.

The young woman was lovely and beautiful.

(Esther 2:7)

Esther was first lovely, then beautiful. A lovely woman appreciates and, with her appreciation, she becomes beautiful by nature. She doesn't need surgery and image consultants for that. Her beauty comes from within. Esther was a godly young woman and just as God appreciated her, she appreciated Him and everything He allowed her to go through.

At first it must have felt strange being swept off into a pagan king's harem, really off target for the plans she had for herself, but she decided to trust in God and embrace the situation that He presented to her at that time. She stood out among all the other young women and the Bible clearly shows that, just so we know that it wasn't because of her extreme beauty that she eventually became queen.

Take a look at the first time she made a difference:

*Thus prepared, each young woman went
to the king, and she was given whatever*

she desired to take with her from the women's quarters to the king's palace. In the evening she went, and in the morning she returned to the second house of the women, to the custody of Shaashgaz, the king's eunuch who kept the concubines. She would not go in to the king again unless the king delighted in her and called for her by name. Now when the turn came for Esther [...] to go in to the king, she requested nothing but what Hegai the king's eunuch, the custodian of the women, advised. And Esther obtained favor in the sight of all who saw her.

(Esther 2:13-15)

If you know you're going to be compared to other women, the first thing you do is find ways to look nicer than the others,

...Esther wasn't exactly the most appreciated of the candidates... She was different from most of them; it wasn't only because she was a Jew... Her difference was within.

to make a big impression, but that's not what Esther did. She could have accessorized with all the luxurious pearls and diamonds offered for her use on the most important night of her life, and yet she decided to take nothing extra (unless what the eunuch advised her). She appreciated who she was, she knew who she was, and above all, she knew in Whom she believed – He would take care of her. That gesture alone made her obtain "favor in the sight of all who saw her"!

> *The king loved Esther more than all the other women, and she obtained grace and favor in his sight more than all the virgins; so he set the royal crown upon her head and made her queen instead of Vashti.*

(Esther 2:17)

Only those who appreciate who they are, and consequently those around them, can have this kind of grace.

It's pretty clear to me through this passage that she wasn't chosen because she was the most beautiful virgin there, but because

"she obtained grace and favor in his sight more than all the virgins"…

Only those who appreciate who they are, and consequently those around them, can have this kind of grace. Esther, as young as she was, with her sad story as an orphan, was a V-Woman. Even the most hard-hearted man, such as King Ahasuerus, was touched by her.

She possessed exactly what his former queen did not. Appreciation.

Is there anything in your life that you've had a hard time appreciating? Why?

How can you start appreciating yourself more? List a few ideas below that you can start implementing from now on.

The **V** woman

My Notes

She's skilled

She stretches out her hands to the distaff,
and her hand holds the spindle.

(Proverbs 31:19)

My good friend Evelyn and I co-founded a young women's exclusive group in our church called "The Sisterhood". The whole idea for the group is to disciple young women to become women of God, who in turn will win the admiration of other young women, who in turn will be introduced to God. The candidates go through a number of tasks, interviews, and tests over a number of weeks and only the top ones make it into the group. The first test comes on paper. They fill out a questionnaire to hand in during their first interview. One of the questions is about their talents and skills and I'm always shocked at how little these

full-of-potential young women know about them-selves… they often think they have none.

The distaff in this verse doesn't just signify a tool used in spinning, but also a term used to describe the feminine side of the family, relating to domestic life. Here's one of my favorite discoveries about the V-Woman: She recognizes her domestic talent!

That's a talent that is exclusive to women and the minute she recognizes it, she begins to excel at it. It's like learning how to read or add. At first it looks impossible; as a little child, you felt as though you were racking your brain just to read a simple word, but once you did it a number of times, it wasn't so hard anymore.

I know a lot of women who think they have no creativity for their home. Their house is never looking good, their first few attempts at decorating their bedroom didn't really turn out as they saw it in the magazine, and so they gave up thinking "this is just not me," accepting that statement as fact.

...one of my favorite discoveries about the V-Woman: She recognizes her domestic talent!

We decide pretty much everything in our lives. If we decide that we can't do something, we won't do it. No matter how hard we try, it's just pointless because we keep on trying to prove that we're right in thinking that we can't. Talk about your worst enemy.

IT'S INNATE

When a woman decides to be a homemaker, that is, when she decides to take care of a home, give it a little of her personality, put things in order, give it a little color, and make it as comfy as she'd like her loved ones to feel, she is able to do it really well. She may get it wrong at first, because she's experimenting and mistakes are a given, but she eventually gets the hang of it. And it's not even because she had to force herself, but because it's in her genes... it's her own natural-born talent to be a homemaker. Her decision only brought out what she'd always had inside.

The V-Woman recognizes the feminine side of her home. She recognizes the things that are natural to her, and she takes advantage of them to bless her family. As far as I can remember in my childhood, my mother has always taken that role in the family - the role of taking care of things at home. No matter how tired she was,

The woman

no matter how many people there were in the house, no matter what time it was, it was her duty to make sure everything was where it was supposed to be.

I never heard her tell my father to wash the dishes or help her around the house… and when it came to us children, she'd teach us but never demand our help, as if to say, "At the end of the day, it's up to me to have everything under control here, so just watch and learn how it's done."

So as soon as I got engaged, I began learning everything there was to know about taking care of a house. From ironing shirts, to washing the bathtub, and cooking with a pressure cooker. I spent hours doing those on my own and when I finally got married, I spent months trying to develop all of those skills.

Sure there were days that I'd get tired of having to iron the same shirts over and over again every week, that I'd look at the kitchen and wish we'd skip dinner for a day, or that I could just sleep in… even the most talented homemaker has her days when she wants to do nothing. But feeling that way is not the norm for her, it's not an everyday thing.

The V-Woman understands her role in the house only too well. She doesn't expect anybody to do it for

her, it's hers and you'd better let her have her way. I took hours to iron my husbands' shirts in the beginning, which would often mean a whole day standing at the ironing board, but eventually I got the hang of it. The skill was there within me all the time, I just had to learn how to develop it, and once I began to work on it, it became a piece of cake!

The same applies to everything else at home. It's all within us, all part of us women. Give it to most men and you'll witness a true male struggle. It's not even fair. If they were forced to live alone, they'd figure out a way to make it work, but it's not their thing.

Many people think that being domestic diminishes a woman. But I think it's a great talent that has become so underrated and unappreciated. Everybody needs a place to live, everybody needs to wear something, every-

...even the most talented homemaker has her days when she wants to do nothing. But feeling that way is not the norm for her, it's not an everyday thing.

body needs to eat something, everybody needs to feel comfortable somewhere... If you can create that atmosphere for these most basic needs of any human being, why would you not see the importance of them? Why would anyone see it as denigrating?

And the beauty of it all is that you can be a great homemaker and still be a great mother, a great wife, a great friend, and a great career woman – something you will hardly see in the male world! Girls, this is exclusive to us! If this isn't a skill, then what is it?

The more we read about the V-Woman, the more we see she's just like us, just more aware of herself. I think this is where most of us fail. We keep trying to find reasons to feel good about ourselves, when all the time, it's been about recognizing our worth, understanding how capable we all are, and how privileged we are for having so much to give to others.

Many people think that being domestic diminishes a woman... it's a great talent that has become so underrated and unappreciated.

SKILLS ARE MEANT TO BE DEVELOPED

Skills are not like tubes of lipstick you can buy off the shelf. Skills are to be developed by those who take an interest in them. If you take an interest in developing this feminine side of you, you'll also start working at it, and as you work, you improve, developing new skills as you go.

When I found myself having to decorate a house from scratch, the first thing I did was to notice things I liked from other people's houses. My mother's house, for example, always had a starting point.

My first major decoration project was my own bedroom when we lived in Cape Town. The house didn't belong to me so I had little say about how it looked, but the bedroom was mine to arrange. So with my little experience in the decorating business, I decided to use my favorite flower, the sunflower, as the main theme. The bedroom was given three colors: blue, yellow, and white.

It looked really sweet and romantic, but after a few months, boy was I tired of those colors! I couldn't stand going into my own bedroom. My husband probably felt the same way but chose not to make a big deal out of it. After all, it was my first try at the distaff.

As soon as we moved from that house, I decided to stay away from blues and yellows, and went for pinky and flowery romantic looks – another flop! Don't get me wrong, these looked wonderful in other people's houses, in the store, and magazines, but for my everyday use, they looked like I had wallpapered everything in the room, not just the walls!

But I didn't let it stop me. Instead of thinking I had no talent, I just kept trying different things instead, and today I enjoy my bedroom. I don't feel the need to move the bed around anymore, I've come to the conclusion that I'm the type of person that likes it clean and neat. White, beige, and some accentuated color somewhere is all I need and I'm happy with that.

EAnd so I enjoy having people over at my house and complimenting me on my decorative style – it gives me a little boost. But I think we all deserve it after so many flops in the past…

If you think you don't have any talents, I tell you, you have at least one, and it's the same one that all other women in the world have – you're a talented homemaker. Whether you develop this talent or not is up to you, but it's freely yours and once you work at it, you'll see what a natural homemaker you can be.

UNKNOWN AND UNAPPRECIATED

There were a couple of women in Jesus' time who recognized their natural homemaking skills and used them to serve the Lord Jesus and His disciples. Since the Lord Jesus wouldn't stay in one particular place for long, they traveled ahead of Him, and arranged everything so that He and His disciples would be able to be properly fed and have a good night's sleep.

> *Now it came to pass, afterward, that He [Jesus] went through every city and village, preaching and bringing the glad tidings of the kingdom of God. And the twelve were with Him, and certain women who had been healed of evil spirits and infirmities — Mary called Magdalene, out of whom had come seven demons, and Joanna the wife of*

I don't feel the need to move the bed around anymore, I've come to the conclusion that I'm the type of person that likes it clean and neat.

 The **woman**

Chuza, Herod's steward, and Susanna, and many others who provided for Him from their substance.

(Luke 8:1-3)

What could these women possibly provide for the Lord Jesus from their own substance? The one thing neither He nor His disciples had: domestic skills. These women followed them around to serve their needs, not because they were their slaves or maids, but because they loved and cared for them. They were touched to see Jesus and the twelve do their work, which had benefited them and others so much, and yet receive little or no appreciation and support from the majority of people who received it.

The disciples didn't take their families with them. They followed the Lord Jesus, who had decided to invest in souls

> If you think you don't have any talents, I tell you, you have at least one, and it's the same one that all other women in the world have – you're a talented homemaker.

instead of having a family of His Own. He deserved appreciation and these women decided they were going to provide it. Their skills were also greatly appreciated, so much so that the Bible mentions them by name as we can see in the verse above.

The Bible doesn't normally give many behind the scenes details, but here you see Luke making it a point to do so. God must have felt deeply honored by these women, just as He feels today when a woman decides, out of her own will, to perform her God-given talents in order to serve Him.

Isn't it amazing how in Bible times, when women were not very valued in society, God appreciated us for even the most basic things we did? This should be enough to knock down any of the snide remarks and arguments today that attack women in the home. If God can appreciate us for cooking, cleaning, and caring for our home and family, why can't we feel great in ourselves for doing it? Why can't we accept this honor given to those who do them well?

What skills have you forgotten to use lately?

What new skills would you like to have?

What can you do to develop these from now on?

The **V** woman

My Notes

_____
_____
_____
_____
_____
_____
_____
_____
_____
_____
_____
_____
_____
_____
_____
_____
_____
_____

She helps

She extends her hand to the poor, yes, she reaches out her hands to the needy.

(Proverbs 31:20)

The poor and needy are not only the ones standing at traffic lights begging for money. We can often make the mistake of thinking that we don't help more people because we don't really have much access to those that need help, when in fact, they are everywhere around us, sometimes even inside our own home. How many people go out of their way to help charities and disaster victims, and yet won't bother to notice the pain in their co-worker's eyes or the lost look on their child's face? Right there in front of you. So much could be done; so much could be fixed…

How many times did you feel alone and didn't even have the strength to ask

for help? If only someone had offered, you would have held onto it with all your might and been grateful to that person for the rest of your life.

The V-Woman understands that. She's always looking for ways to help someone in need, whoever he or she is. Sometimes all the person needs is a smile, a word of encouragement, or even a bag of clothes. If you have it, why not spare it?

A woman who knows how to help is a rarity in this selfish world. Most people are always looking for ways to get something for themselves, they don't want to give or lose, only to gain. The more you give them, the more they want to drain you of all you've got.

> A woman who knows how to help is a rarity in this selfish world. Most people are always looking for ways to get something for themselves...

When I began writing this book, I encountered a number of blocks in my way; not the usual "writer's block." These were different, more in-your-face kinds. I have a daily blog,

which I cherish very much. But as time went by and the book was given the least of my time and effort because of the blog and my other responsibilities I hold as a pastor's wife, mother, mentor, and my other day to day roles , I came to an abrupt decision. I was going to have to let go of some things in order to focus better on the book.

And as usual, I vented my frustrations on my blog. I didn't think my readers would mind if I told them that I was going to put the blogs and advice on pause for a while. I didn't want to look like a "sensitive artist," but at the same time I wanted to explain how I felt, and how to deal with high-priority projects when we struggle with concentration.

Believe it or not, that was one of the blogs in which I was most attacked. Most of my faithful readers did understand and offered me support; but to my disappointment, some who chose to remain anonymous were upset with my decision.

At first I felt hurt, but decided to leave it at that. After all, those who are godly understand each other. So I began posting old articles from 2007, which I'm sure for most of my blog readers, were just as new since the blog was only created in 2008. These articles had come out in some of our church magazines and newspapers,

and were still pretty helpful and good enough to be posted again.

A few weeks later, I got a comment that almost knocked me off my chair: "I already read this article a long time ago. Why do you keep on posting old articles here? I want to read new ones, come on!"

It's funny how some people don't realize that they're receiving so much for free yet demand so much more at the same price. The more you give, the more people want to take from you, that's just how life is. But if you stop giving, thinking that it will stop others from being spoiled, you yourself will stop receiving altogether.

These frustrated blog readers enjoyed being on the receiving end of what I had to give. But when they had a chance to give back some support, instead of taking the advice they had been given all along, they didn't reach out to help, they didn't understand, they didn't care.

The world will do this to you, but the key is to never ever let it get the better of you. I was hurt at first, but I chose to let go of those feelings and keep on giving despite the fact that some who received so much didn't appreciate it one bit. We shouldn't help or give because we'll get something back, we should do it because it's the right thing to do.

The V-Woman helps because it's the right thing to do. Whether she's recognized for it or not, she'll always give a helping hand, always be there when you need her, always be a person you can count on. That's where most of her beauty comes from.

People who can give without recognition are rare, and when you find them, you love them without even knowing them personally. They give demanding nothing. From time to time the media will heap praises on some big name in business, entertainment, or politics who donated big money to charity. But is that really selfless? If you're rich, you're expected to donate large amounts to charity. Your name gets some good PR, and your reputation shoots through the roof. An investment like that is worth some spare change.

There's nothing really admirable about high profile acts of charity that are often given only to stimulate some sort of return: huge tax breaks, new business

> We shouldn't help or give because we'll get something back, we should do it because it's the right thing to do.

deals, an image boost for unscrupulous corporations. But not so for the unseen acts of kindness you can do for those who can't give you anything in return. That's when God becomes your reward. That's when you become a V-Woman – far more precious than the most expensive ruby in the world.

God feels obliged to reward those who follow His example of giving, because He knows what it's like to be unappreciated. He knows how it feels when people only want to take and never give anything back. God goes through this every single minute of every single day… And yet, He's always there, available to anyone who calls on Him. The V-Woman lives her life according to God's ways and so she faithfully takes on of all His traits.

God feels obliged to reward those who follow His example of giving, because He knows what it's like to be unappreciated.

NO PROSPECTS, JUST ROUTINE

Rebekah was a young V-Woman who was tremendously blessed by the simple understanding of this truth. She was young and single, from a family living in the desert, without much prospect for the future except to keep doing what her predecessors had always done. As most women did then, Rebekah's job was to draw a day's supply of water for the household and carry it home. It was a harsh routine, carrying water from afar for everyone including the animals. Women those days must have had some really strong muscles!

One particular day, a stranger came running up to her at the well. Rebekah may have felt frightened at first, just as anyone would have with a stranger appearing in a remote place like that.

> *And the servant ran to meet her and said, "Please let me drink a little water from your pitcher." So she said, "Drink, my lord." Then she quickly let her pitcher down to her hand, and gave him a drink.*

(Genesis 24:17,18)

She obviously decided to keep her cool, and pretend she wasn't afraid, as you and I would have done in that situation. But what she did next was something uncommon, which is exactly what made all the difference to Rebekah's future:

The *V* woman

*And when she had finished giving him
a drink, she said, "I will draw water for
your camels also, until they have finished
drinking." Then she quickly emptied her
pitcher into the trough, ran back to the
well to draw water, and drew for all his
camels. And the man, wondering at her,
remained silent so as to know whether
the LORD had made his journey pros-
perous or not. So it was, when the camels had finished drinking, that the man
took a golden nose ring weighing half a
shekel, and two bracelets for her wrists
weighing ten shekels of gold, and said,
"Whose daughter are you?"*

(Genesis 24:19-23)

So Rebekah watered the stranger's camels. This
man had 10 camels, and each camel can drink up to
50 gallons… That wasn't exactly a glass of water! She
really went out of her way to help a stranger — something unheard of, something that shows an amazing
amount of respect. Here you have a young inexperienced woman teaching us all a lesson on how to become a V-Woman by simply helping a total stranger.

The Bible even says that he was "wondering at her" – what a sight! Perhaps dozens of other women had gone to that very well to draw water, but Rebekah was different from them all. She helped the man, not only in attending to his request, but over and above what he had not requested.

Little did she know that this man held a whole new future for her. He had made a vow before God that the woman who would offer to give water to his camels would be the one God chooses to be a suitable wife for his master Isaac, Abraham's son of the promise. From them would come God's nation of Israel.

One act of giving can do wonders. It can change hearts, transform minds, start a new beginning and add a happily ever after to the end. One act. Now imagine loads of them? Imagine if you actually start enjoying the thrill of

> One act of giving can do wonders. It can change hearts, transform minds, start a new beginning and add a happily ever after to the end.

giving and helping others, and you start doing it over and over again… you'll be like a rose in the middle of the desert, just as Rebekah was, so beautiful and impossible to go unnoticed.

The V-Woman doesn't need to be recognized internationally or by the media. In fact, they barely ever pay her any attention. The V-Woman is recognized by those of her own world – people in her church, her friends, in school, at home, at work, and even in the neighborhood. They may not say it to her face, but they're all aware of her and they all secretly admire her from afar… How can they not? A rose in the desert is just too hard to miss!

How can you start a habit of helping and giving to others without asking anything in return?

Who could these people be? Where and how would you start off?

The V-Woman
doesn't need to
be recognized
internationally or
by the media.

My Notes

She plans

She is not afraid of snow for her house-hold, for all her household is clothed with scarlet.

(Proverbs 31:21)

S now in those days must have been hard. Imagine having no snow plows clearing the roads and spreading salt, no central heating, no insulation, and no 4x4s with snow tires. If it snowed, you were homebound. That meant, no food or water or travel. And if supplies ran out…

The V-Woman thought ahead. Her family was well taken care of because she made plans for all kinds of situations. This is a little recognized characteristic that can be a lifesaver. People like to live life as it comes. If it's harsh, they deal with it there and then. Since they hardly ever prepare, they suffer.

Normally people who don't plan are people who depend on others. They don't know how to drive because someone else drives for them. They don't know how to cook because someone else does it for them. They don't know how to be a mother because someone else takes the job off their hands… they don't plan, they don't care, they don't like to think about it.

Sure they can get away with it while someone else does it for them, but for how long? How long will others have to go out of their way to come to their rescue? Life is too short. If you don't want to plan ahead, don't become an obstacle for those who do.

THE PICTURE IN YOUR MIND

My mother tells me that I was still in her womb when she pictured my face in her mind. She says I turned out to be just like she had pictured back then. That was nice to hear! A simple mental pic-

> Every time you plan, your future can be molded to turn out the way you want.

ture of how I'd be… 'Big deal', somebody might say. But as strange as it sounds, it actually happened. It's that simple kind of faith that visualizes a dream, and determines that it is more than a dream – it's real. This kind of planning makes things happen all the time… Every time you plan, your future can be molded to turn out the way you want.

Jacob did something similar. He had made an agreement with his father-in-law who was also his boss, that all the spotted sheep and goats would be his. And upon that agreement, the Bible says that:

> *"Took fresh-cut branches from poplar, almond and plane trees and made white stripes on them by peeling the bark and exposing the white inner wood of the branches. Then he placed the peeled branches in all the watering troughs, so that they would be directly in front of the flocks when they came to drink. When the flocks were in heat and came to drink, they mated in front of the branches. And they bore young that were streaked or speckled or spotted"*

(Genesis 30:37-39 NIV)

 The woman

Okay, so Jacob was being clever here, but think of how interesting the whole concept is. The animals would look at an image and later on give birth to off-spring that looked like that image!

This means that if you want to get anywhere, you've got to see it first in your mind. A career, becoming a homeowner, having a family, and even getting the body you dream of. It must first be clear in your mind. If you can't see it, you won't get it.

Many years ago when I was newly married, I sacrificed my right to give birth, something very dear to most of us women. I had no children and I gave up the right to have any as a vow to God. Up until that moment, I had always dreamed of becoming a mother and having my own children, but one day my goal changed into a whole different one. I'd have spiritual children instead of physical ones, something that I desired even more. I didn't know how that would happen but I had an inexplicable assurance inside of me that it was God's dream for me.

God honored me for that, and though a few years later we adopted a 4-year-old, I was still blessed for sacrificing my personal dreams for God's dreams. I

feel honored today when I hear young and older women call me their spiritual mother…

God is the biggest supporter of our dreams. He tells us we can achieve whatever we believe. It was probably He who originally put that dream of yours inside of you.

Like any good parent, God wants to see us becoming the best we can be. His plans for us are much better than we can ever imagine, but there's only one thing that stops Him from fulfilling them: our disbelief.

When we believe, we see it in our minds. Even though circumstances around us may be saying "no way", we keep believing regardless. It's a clear image of what we want and where we want to go.

A very smart and pleasant woman came to talk to me in church one day. She had gone through a lot of issues in her past, abuse, neglect, and all sorts of traumas that are hard to

> God is the biggest supporter of our dreams. He tells us we can achieve whatever we believe.

shake off. She wanted to move on in life, marry someone, raise a family, and be happy. But at the same time, she struggled with all that had happened in her past, as if she was tied to it so tightly that she could never be free from it.

"How do I let go of the past?" she asked after hearing so much about it in church.

I looked at her and deep inside I prayed that God would give me the answer to that question; I hadn't gone through even 5% of what she had. How could I help her with that one? And that's when He came to our rescue and I said: "Plan your future."

If you want to let go of your past, you need to start looking away from it and the only way that can be done is by looking forward, towards what's yet to come.

> If you want to let go of your past, you need to start looking away from it and the only way that can be done is by looking forward...

The worse your past, the more chances you have of a greater future.

Do you know why? Because you're stronger than the average woman who hasn't gone through what you have. If you got yourself here, after all that has happened to you, how would you rate yourself? I'd give you all 5 stars!

Think of any of the most inspiring true stories you know. Did the main character sail through life with no trouble at all? The main reason why the story is inspiring is exactly because that person went through so much. The worse his life, the more significant his success. That person decided to use his past to change his future, to plan a whole different future for himself. And with that, he created a kind of life worthy of a best-seller.

I have observed a fact of life: the more potential you have, the higher the price you pay. If you're going far, you're bound to have more obstacles than if you weren't really going anywhere.

KNOWN FOR THE WRONG REASONS

Rahab's story is quite remarkable. She was a ceremonial prostitute, a common feature in religions that worshiped gods or goddesses of fertility. She lived in

the filth of that kind of life, day in and day out. She endured being used and abused – in the name of a god – just to survive. She first heard about the God of the Bible when some really bad news spread through her land of Jericho. They were on the verge of being attacked by Israel, a strong nation, who was led by a God who actually worked miracles and cared about His people.

She began hearing stories of this God, and the more she heard, the more hope of a better life began growing in her soul. Nobody else in Jericho saw it that way. They were just scared and angry. No one else reasoned intelligently as she did. "Why not join this God who seems to be real and change our fortune too?" she must have thought.

No doubt God saw Rahab's interest in Him because two of His spies soon came to her inn and she immediately recognized they weren't just foreigners. They were different; they were from Israel. God was giving her the chance of a lifetime, a golden opportunity to save herself from her past and create a new future.

Rahab helped the two spies by hiding them from the people of her town, who had also noticed them.

(People who belong to God often stand out in a crowd. They're just so different, a difference that can't be described with mere words.)

In return, she asked for help from the spies: To spare her and her family when they attacked and be taken by the nation of Israel as refugees. And they agreed. And as Israel attacked Jericho, Rahab and her family were securely taken to a new country, a new beginning, a new life. Why Rahab of all people? Why not the righteous neighbor to the left or the perfect housewife who lived on the same street?

Because no one believed. No one planned.

When you believe, you plan. That's as simple as it gets. When you don't believe, you find excuses as to why you shouldn't plan. You're a foreigner, you're not educated, you're not rich, you're not good enough, you're not mature, you're not

...God saw Rahab's interest in Him... God was giving her the chance of a lifetime... to save herself from her past and create a new future.

The woman

old enough, you're not perfect, you're not, you're not, you're not! Oh how easy it is to just not believe…

But when we believe, we don't care about what we don't have, what we're not, and what we've been through. It's as if we're ignorant about everything that makes sense.

It's interesting that many of us did this when growing up. We used to play make-believe all the time. I used to pretend that I was my father's secretary and that I was very good at it. I didn't care that I didn't really know the job or that I was too young for the job. All I cared about was that I was doing what I liked to do. And I could do or be anything I wanted by using my imagination.

When you believe, you plan. That's as simple as it gets. When you don't believe, you find excuses as to why you shouldn't plan.

Rahab wanted a new beginning. She wanted to have a family of her own, without having to carry the reputation that had shamed her all those years.

She didn't know how but she believed. She didn't have what it took to begin a new life on her own, but she did hear that Israel had a God that performed miracles. And that's just what she needed.

A lot of women in her shoes would have probably given up on life or never done anything too risky to get out. Betraying their own country? Take a stand against the people who used and abused them for so long? Oh no, they'd rather be committed to that worthless life they were accustomed to.

Isn't that what many of us do as well? We remain faithful to the very things that have tormented us for years. Faithful to the idea that we've always held about ourselves that we'll never be anything in life. We keep telling ourselves the same thing over and over again, so we won't hope, and won't expect anything better.

The V-Woman is not afraid to believe and so she plans, without the need of a good argument to do it. She just does it. Rahab planned a new life in a new country, with a new God, and so she got it. Soon after her arrival in Israel, she married an Israelite, who wasn't just any old Joe, but a husband who made her a very important ancestor for

The woman

us all. Rahab was included in the lineage of the Lord Jesus!

Just like the V-Woman in Proverbs 31, Rahab saved her whole family because she was not afraid of what was yet to come; she believed, and so she planned.

How do you see yourself?

What are your plans?

Where do you see yourself in a few years?

My Notes

She takes care of herself

She makes tapestry for herself; Her clothing is fine linen and purple.

(Proverbs 31:22)

As little girls, we can grow up thinking we're princesses worthy of everyone's attention. Simple high heeled sandals or a shiny necklace is enough to make us feel like the most beautiful girl on the block! Then we grow up and start reading magazines, watching movies and TV shows, and understanding what their gospel of "true beauty" is about. We look at our bodies and suddenly realize we don't belong in that group. Ideas slap us in the face like, "Only long slender legs look stunning," "Blondes have more fun," "Shrink to a size 0 and you'll look great like her," "So-and-so is the most beautiful woman in the world. Too bad you're noth-

The *V* woman

ing like her," and "Wrinkles, bags, and sags? Girl, go do something about your face!"

Then we look in the mirror and the self-attack begins.

Who gave the media the power to say what's beautiful and what's not? Did you? I certainly didn't! We should be the ones who decide what's beautiful for us.

That's where the V-Woman comes in. This woman never ceases to amaze me. She cares for her family, her finances, her home, people in need, and still she has time to care for herself. Here's something you rarely see nowadays… It's usually one or the other. The wonderful caring woman who feeds the homeless and serves in her church but is out of shape and wears old-fashioned clothes, or the image-conscious social climber who lives for her looks at the expense of her home and family. Sometimes I ask myself what happened to women throughout the years that made us fall so far away from our tree. We can do this; we have always done this in the past, before industrialization… could this be some-

> Who gave the media the power to say what's beautiful and what's not?

thing to do with the feminist movement that swept us away from our original values?

The V-Woman lived in a pre-feminist time, and through all that we've read so far, she seemed quite happy that way. She took care of herself. Did you know that when you're happy inside, you also take better care of yourself?

Think of the times when you were sick and how hard it was for you to find the best outfit that day, just because you just weren't in the mood. It's all linked. If you're sad, you withdraw from others, and probably wear some dark lifeless outfit without even realizing it. It's in your subconscious, too deep to notice.

So the secret of taking care of yourself begins with your attitude. It's not enough for you to say you'll start doing it now and hope for the best. You need to be conscious of why you should take care of yourself first.

DO IT FOR YOURSELF

First things first. If you don't take care of yourself, who will? Just like quenching your thirst, if you don't drink water, nobody can do it for you. Taking care of yourself is a basic need. You shouldn't do it because

your husband or your friend told you so, you should do it for yourself. They're your looks. It's your life. People who take care of their looks because of anything other than themselves often do it badly.

This explains the candid camera pictures of beautiful celebrities looking really unkempt for a simple day in the park. They're beautiful when they know they'll be in front of the cameras, but not for themselves; it's as if they say, *"I'm not working today so I reserve the right to look ugly."*

Another reason why you should take care of yourself is the message you give out to people around you. Some wives may not realize it but they blast out this message to their husbands: You'd better not care about my looks now that I'm finally married and gaining weight! Poor guys… they thought they had married a woman who cared about herself, but instead she just loves her comfort.

Sure, being on the pill or the new baby may have contributed to the weight gain. But you did contribute plenty on your own, be honest. Don't blame the meds or the baby. You know when you're going overboard. An extra serving here and there, telling yourself that you'll only do it this time (just like the last few times), that's all.

Take care of yourself for you first, and then because you appreciate others around you, especially your spouse, if you're married. Unlike the majority of women who think they only have to look their best before they get married, if you took care of yourself before, you need to double the efforts now that you have the man of your dreams.

As a married woman, you belong to your husband just as he belongs to you. Don't you want him to feel proud of having you next to him, to make him look good before his peers, and to keep finding you interesting and attractive with age?

I've always done what I could to make sure that if my husband ever looked at another woman, he'd think to himself, *"Why would I need that cheap Ford? I have a Porsche at home!"*

Beauty does come from within. People we love can look gorgeous or extremely handsome, and it's not always entirely due to their looks, but because of whom

> Take care of yourself for you first, and then because you appreciate others around you...

we know they are. However, that doesn't mean beauty should only remain within. Beauty is to be shown and to be admired. Who doesn't love to look at beautiful things?

Okay, so now you know you need to take care of yourself and why it is good for you. Now the next question everyone always asks me is: How do I start?

First ask the question, "What do people who love themselves do?" They show it. They work hard at it. They learn how to do it and they let it show by the way they look.

MAKING IT HAPPEN

People we love can look gorgeous... it's not always entirely due to their looks, but because of whom we know they are.

How about a healthy diet and daily exercises for starters? What if you changed your hairstyle as a demonstration of a new you that's emerging? What if, instead of that old pair of jeans so

worn out that they walk around the house by themselves when you're not looking, you wear a dress in a bolder color just for the fun of it? Then add a couple of extra accessories to complete a look you never thought to try. Why not?

You don't need to go for a professional makeover somewhere that lasts for a day or two and then washes off. You can do it today, and learn how to make it a habit – right now as a matter of fact. Nowadays, you don't need to have loads of money to look great. All you need is the will to do it.

I can already predict what's about to happen as you begin this process… you'll start enjoying it! You'll want to do it more and more. You'll start looking forward to the time you dress up in the morning!

Taking good care of yourself will only do you good. It's fun, exciting, and extremely rewarding. When I woke up to this fact, it was as if I had been revived – no more clothes that made me look old and no more wig-like haircuts. I started taking the time to do my nails every week (by myself by the way), go bolder with the colors I wore, and try something different with my hair every week. As I started to enjoy what I saw, I started to care more, until it became a daily routine. If you can care for yourself, then you can care for others.

Caring about your beauty is not rocket science as many women think it is. Creativity is the key, so work with that side of your brain. Every time you get a chance to grab a magazine or watch TV, notice the make-up, the color combinations, the hairstyles, and basically anything that you can see. As I said before, the media can't dictate to us what is beautiful and what is not, but it doesn't mean we can't learn from them with wisdom and discretion. Notice that not everything is appropriate or even nice, but you can glean a lot of hints from simple make-up advertisements.

1. **You can start by using what you have.** You don't really have to spend money if you're just a bit creative with what you have right now. If you'll just look in your closet and spot the things you can mix and match – you'll already look different.

2. **You should also be able to identify** your best features and invest in them.

3. **You can be bold with your looks.** Skirts, dark and bold colors, and accessories can be some of your first bold moves. It's amazing how bold colors will bring out a whole new you...

Once you start taking the extra time each morning, you start enjoying the challenge. You'll obviously

make mistakes now and again because this is a new thing, a new phase, a new you. You won't know your style immediately, but that's completely normal.

I don't get it when I hear people say they can't be creative. It's like saying they can't learn anything new. Anybody, at any age and from any background has the ability to be creative – unless they don't want to be. You don't have to get it right the first time, but you can certainly get better at it with time.

If you're like most women I know, you probably take too much time trying to figure out what to wear in the morning and after you do, you probably think it's not good enough and you wish you weren't so late to go back and try something else. But since you are, you leave home feeling exactly the same as the way you're dressed – rushed!

Contrary to what some of us think, mornings were not made just to make life harder for us. I know it feels like the morning

> Caring about your beauty is not rocket science as many women think it is.

hours are so rushed, but they're not – we are. The se-cret to getting dressed in the morning on time is by working on these three steps:

1. **Organize your closet.** You must be able to see every-thing you have at once. If you have clothes behind other clothes, accessories inside drawers, and shoes inside box-es, then you're a heroine if you manage to figure out an out-fit! One way of simplifying things is by placing everything right where you can see it. First, I like to hang all of the same types of clothing (skirts, tops, dresses, etc.) together. Then I organize them by color. Then I place all my shoes in transparent boxes so I can see them all (if I had the closet of my dreams, I'd have a wall just for them!). Then I have my belts and scarves hanging next to my necklaces. This way, I see everything I have and can easily mix and match.

2. **Prepare it the night before.** If you know you're not going to have enough time in the morning to fix your hair, makeup and still find an outfit – choose the outfit before you go to sleep. That way, it's one

Anybody, at any age and from any background has the ability to be creative...

less thing to do in the morning and because you have some time on your hands, you can probably discover something really creative and different to wear the next day if you've already done step 1.

3. **Be creative with your hair.** If you're having a bad hair day, why not make an elegant pony tail or simply wear a headband? Accessories help women pretend to have taken a long time to get ready in the morning… so let's enjoy them!

JUDGED AND UNNOTICED

Abishag is a name you probably never noticed in the Bible. She's mentioned once, in one verse, as if by chance. But since we all know there are no coincidences when it comes to God, this young woman's short description is one to teach and speak about.

At the time, King David was very old, and though he had hundreds of wives at his beck and call, it's interesting to note that his servants had to come up with a plan in order to keep him warm during the night. One wonders why… How can such a successful man like King David, with plenty of spare wives to choose from, be all alone during the night?

Could it be that his wives had already given up their role in his life and were now only enjoying the benefits of palace life? I don't know, but it's certainly strange to read this about David in his old age.

> *Therefore his servants said to him, "Let a young woman, a virgin, be sought for our lord the king, and let her stand before the king, and let her care for him; and let her lie in your bosom, that our lord the king may be warm." So they sought for a lovely young woman throughout all the territory of Israel, and found Abishag the Shunammite, and brought her to the king. The young woman was very lovely; and she cared for the king, and served him; but the king did not know her.*

(1 Kings 1:2-4)

Abishag was chosen from among the best of the best and the only description that we have from these verses of her is that she was very lovely. What do you think King David's servants saw in this young virgin in order to trust her to take care of their king?

I think we can safely say that when one knows how to take care of oneself, one also knows how to take care of others. She was lovely, and the only way they could have known that about her was by the way she looked. You don't have to be the prettiest woman on the block, but you do owe it to yourself to at least take the best possible care of the way you look. People enjoy being around those who enjoy themselves. They exude an air of contentment that makes their presence desirable and pleasant.

The Bible may not mention Abishag much, but it mentions her. And for sure, there's a reason why. She was important to David. Her lovely nature made up for what he didn't have in his old age. She served him well, not in a sexual way, but in a womanly way…

How have you taken care of yourself lately?

What could you start doing differently from now on?

> You don't have to be the prettiest woman on the block, but you do owe it to yourself to at least take the best possible care of the way you look.

My Notes

_____
_____
_____
_____
_____
_____
_____
_____
_____
_____
_____
_____
_____
_____
_____
_____
_____
_____
_____
_____
_____

She's popular

Her husband is known in the gates, when
he sits among the elders of the land.

(Proverbs 31:23)

*I*magine being married to someone everyone admires. That's what it was like
for the V-Woman's husband. He was
popular, and his wife had a direct hand
in helping him to become great. Not that
he wasn't already a great guy, but let's
face it: he made a big investment when he married
her. He married up!

Women have the ability to do either
one of these two things: add or take away.
There's no way you can simply keep
things the way they've always been when
you are around others. You either influence them for better or for worse. Now if
you think about it, that's a lot of power.

When you're married, this power multiplies. If you're not adding, you're probably taking away from your husband's life. If you're not representing him well, you're representing him badly. If you're not lifting him up, you're putting him down... and when you have children, this power grows even more. Women are the ones who set the tone of their family atmosphere at home.

A father may be angry and the children distant, but if the mother is peaceful, they can still sit down and eat a meal together. On the other hand, if the father is in the mood for some family time, the children are craving attention, but the mother is angry, there's no way you'll see them enjoy a meal together. The mother is the link to their unity, and if that link is broken, the family does not connect.

It is scary to think that you can be the one who spoils everything for your

> A father may be
> angry and the
> children distant,
> but if the mother is
> peaceful, they can still
> sit down and eat
> a meal together.

family; it may seem far-fetched, but test it and see. Notice who usually determines the atmosphere in your house.

You'd think that men would just choose not to rely on women for the happiness in their home, but their need for us is in their genes. Back when Adam had just been created and had all the power in the world to do whatever he wanted, when he walked with God in the Garden and had Him as his Best Friend, he still lacked this… and God knew it.

INSECURE AND NAÏVE

God had to create a helper for Adam – a woman, Eve.

> *And the LORD God said, "It is not good that man should be alone; I will make him a helper comparable to him." Out of the ground the LORD God formed every beast of the field and every bird of the air, and brought them to Adam to see what he would call them. And whatever Adam called each living creature, that was its name. So Adam gave names to all cattle, to the birds of the air, and to every beast*

of the field. But for Adam there was not
found a helper comparable to him.

(Genesis 2:18-20)

We came about out of a need. We weren't a decorative ornament in God's beautiful new creation; we
were the missing piece of it all. He first created man
and even had him busy at work for awhile, but as soon
as God saw Adam's inexplicable need for a helper,
He came to his rescue. God is always in tune with our
needs, even when we don't understand them ourselves.

He had to create someone who would be comparable to Adam, someone who would fit right in with
His best creation of all, and together, form an even
better creation – a family. Let's read Genesis 2:21-
25 together:

And the LORD God caused a deep sleep
to fall on Adam, and he slept; and He
took one of his ribs, and closed up the
flesh in its place. Then the rib which the
LORD God had taken from man He
made into a woman, and He brought her
to the man.

(Genesis 2:21,22)

God didn't really have to form us out of a man's rib, did He? He could have done it the way He made Adam. There was no need for Adam to go through all the trouble of having a rib removed from his side. Adam could still be perfect, with all his ribs in place, and have a woman for his wife, but that wasn't how it happened. God chose the hard way for a reason.

God wanted the woman to come out of man; He wanted them to be linked in a deeper way than just by words.

> *And Adam said: "This is now bone of my bones, and flesh of my flesh; she shall be called Woman, because she was taken out of Man." Therefore a man shall leave his father and mother and be joined to his wife, and they shall become one flesh. And they were both naked, the man and his wife, and were not ashamed.*
>
> (Genesis 2:23-25)

God wanted the woman to come out of man; He wanted them to be linked...

The woman

You can imagine how delighted Adam must have felt when he looked at Eve for the first time. He must have quickly forgotten the missing rib! He immediately called her Woman, a reminder to him that she was taken out of him and made for him, exclusively. Eve was custom-made for Adam, just like all women have been custom-made for men.

We have what they need, and if we use what we have wisely, we'll surely be one flesh. And when that happens, there's no shame; man and woman may be totally different from one another, but they'll still complete one another.

Everything that God created was perfect, including the fact that we're so different from men while, at the same time, we're so attracted to each other.

> We have what they (men) need, and if we use what we have wisely, we'll surely be one flesh.

A man can live as a bachelor for most of his life, but what he's really doing is living in denial; he's hurt and the best way he thinks of dealing with that disappointment from his past is to avoid commitment.

A woman can work hard to be independent and self-sufficient, and still feel as though she's being deprived of something. What she really wants, if she can find it, is to rely on a real man; she yearns to complete a man, even if that's secretly stashed away in her subconscious.

Every woman can be popular and make a man popular when she understands her role in his life. Since Eve had no background to rely on, she accepted her role in Adam's life immediately. She was to help him, to give him support, and to add to his life, just like he had added so much to hers.

Eve is the most influential woman in the Bible; she was the first woman ever created. She saw what we have never been able to see: she lived life before sin. She walked with God side by side until the day she decided to do something that humanity paid the price for ever since. We have all blamed her at one time or another – it is hard not to!

Just when Eve had it all going for her, she listened to God's number one enemy for the first time. I'm sure that the devil had been trying to get to Adam for a long

time with no success. But as he watched Adam and Eve live in harmony, he must have noticed how much influence Eve had on Adam's decisions… he must have noticed how Adam relied on Eve in an unspoken way.

And without further ado, he changed his target to Eve. If he could get to her, he had no doubt he could get to Adam too.

As he watched Eve more closely, he began to notice her desire to learn more, know more, have more, get more, and be more. She was different from Adam. Adam was all about working hard and benefiting from the fruit of his work, while Eve was more into doing it all with a touch of emotion. She liked to feel things, and got a thrill out of those emotions she'd often have.

When the devil came up with his master plan of using a serpent to talk sweetly with Eve, he knew how easy it was all going to be; and because God could not interfere with His new babies' free will, He was left to watch from the sidelines and grieve…

> *Now the serpent was more cunning than any beast of the field which the LORD God had made. And he said to the woman, "Has God indeed said, 'You shall not*

eat of every tree of the garden'?" And the woman said to the serpent, "We may eat the fruit of the trees of the garden; but of the fruit of the tree which is in the midst of the garden, God has said, 'You shall not eat it, nor shall you touch it, lest you die.'"

(Genesis 3:1-3)

All the serpent needed to do was, first, become Eve's friend – and we all know how easy it is to make friends with a naïve girl... We love making new friends, we love creating networks... Second, all the dreadful little beast had to do was feed her a few ideas. They didn't have to be true; they just had to make her react to them somehow, lead her to do something – that's all.

Then the serpent said to the woman, "You will not surely die. For God knows that in

All the serpent needed to do was... become Eve's friend... we all know how easy it is to make friends with a naïve girl...

The woman

the day you eat of it your eyes will be opened, and you will be like God, knowing good and evil.".

(Genesis 3:4,5)

Eve didn't stop and think about the serpent's nonsense; she just let her emotions do the thinking: "Yes, yes... I don't think God really meant what He said... it might be nice for us to know more about good and evil... God will understand..."

So when the woman saw that the tree was good for food, that it was pleasant to the eyes, and a tree desirable to make one wise, she took of its fruit and ate.

(Genesis 3:6)

Eve didn't stop and think about the serpent's nonsense; she just let her emotions do the thinking...

Just like that. Eve didn't take time to think about it, she didn't talk to her husband about it, she just saw, took, and ate from the tree – a real déjà vu for some of us. How many times have we done the same thing? We see something, we don't think about it, we just go ahead and do it, and then think about it later, after the damage has already been done.

Women are often driven by their emotions. We have a hard time being rational, not because we can't, but because we want to feel first. Is it any wonder most TV commercials are targeted at women. We don't care that we can't afford it, or that we don't really need it, we want it.

And as the devil suspected, Eve didn't just take it for herself, "she also gave to her husband with her, and he ate" (Genesis 3:6).

So typical of us. I don't think she meant to hurt Adam. She just wanted to share, as we often do. We like to share things. We want to vent. We want to unburden how we feel and so we take it to someone else who can potentially be harmed by what we say without us even realizing it.

You'd think that Adam would know better than to just accept whatever Eve handed him. He'd been alive longer than her, he should have known, he should have helped her. But that's the thing, men are easily influenced by women – and they don't even re-

alize it. Adam didn't see it and, when he came to his senses, he had already tasted the fruit. His blessing was already gone.

> *Then the eyes of both of them were opened, and they knew that they were naked; and they sewed fig leaves together and made themselves coverings.*

(Genesis 3:7)

Everything changed from that day onwards. If they had been the only ones who suffered loss because of that horrible mistake, it wouldn't have been so bad... but we all lost out. Every one of us suffers today because of that one incident, that one case of poor judgment due to one woman's bad influence.

Check out these two powerful verses:

> *An excellent wife is the crown of her husband, but she who causes shame is like rottenness in his bones.*

(Proverbs 12:4)

> *The wise woman builds her house, but the foolish pulls it down with her hands.*

(Proverbs 14:1)

There's no middle ground: either you're a wise and excellent wife, or you are foolish and rottenness in your husband's bones. That's how influential you can be.

The Bible only attributes this power to women – not to men.

The V-Woman understands this quite well. She knows how popular and influential she is, how significant her opinions are, what an impact her moods can have, and so she takes advantage of them to uplift those around her.

What can you do to use this power of influence you have to be a blessing to those around you?

How can you avoid being a negative influence to your family from now on?

...men are easily influenced by women – and they don't even realize it.

The *V* woman

My Notes

_____
_____
_____
_____
_____
_____
_____
_____
_____
_____
_____
_____
_____
_____
_____
_____
_____

She's creative

She makes linen garments and sells them,
and supplies sashes for the merchants.

(Proverbs 31:24)

*I*f you read all the verses that talk about the V-Woman, you'll conclude that some of them are similar. But then again, what if they're not? They may seem at first glance to be saying the same thing, but look deeper and you'll see they mean something significantly different.

When she looked around and saw that linen was the new IN thing, she didn't miss the opportunity. Make linen garments, wear them, sell them, and while you're at it, why not make some cute sashes that people won't be able to resist buying?

In other words, the V-Woman was creative. She didn't take long to come up with ideas, which is a very nice trait for us to have these days, especially when we are tempted to waste hours at a time on Facebook, MySpace, Twitter, MSN, Orkut, and so on.

We need to think fast and be creative. It's not that we shouldn't go online and browse or chat once in a while; but when these things take away our precious time, we end up only accomplishing the daily basics. We lack time for creativity.

Make sure everything you do has a reason. If you're reading this book, it's because you want to be a better woman. If you're on Facebook, it's because you want to share good things with others, and who knows, glorify our Lord Jesus while at it.

A woman who is creative is also bold, and may sometimes seem extravagant, without meaning to. She's creative in everything she does. If she's getting dressed in the morning, she's creative. If she's tidying up

> If you're reading this book, it's because you want to be a better woman.

her home, she's creative. If she's going out with a friend, she'll be creative there too. In short, she uses her creativity in everything she does and anywhere she goes.

This is actually a nice tip for people who get bored easily. The minute you start using your creativity to enjoy the things you do, you cause your usual routine to come to a halt, and fun comes running towards you.

The V-Woman is fun and never boring. She's always evolving, always going for something new and exciting; and because of that, people are attracted to her. She's that kind of friend who will push you to become bold and different, and feel good while doing it.

CREATIVITY: KILLS BOREDOM, OPENS COUNTLESS DOORS

I had to develop this side of me in order to avoid getting stuck in one of the things I truly despise: routine. At 17, I married the man of my dreams, and started the life I had planned for myself since I was a child. I married a pastor and that meant living the rest of my life as an offering to God on the Altar, serving others, and never again living for myself, my family, or for my own personal desires.

The woman

In the beginning, it was all new for me. Though I had been raised as a pastor's daughter, it was still different being married to one. It was fun; I got myself busy learning how to take care of a home and being a good wife for my husband.

There was always something new every week: some exciting event happening in our church, some new evangelization plans, new people who had joined, new pastors' wives who had arrived, new miracles to share, and new insights from the Word of God we couldn't wait to spread. I began helping my husband more and more in his ministry. I played the keyboard in church, helped around the office, and organized the rooms of old churches. I became a busy pastor's wife and I loved it.

But as soon as my son arrived, I put all of the above on hold and focused all of my time and effort on him. And boy, that was hard!

I'd stay home all day while all my friends were working hard in church and enjoying their challenges together. I was alone. I began being the last one to hear about things that happened, and that feeling of isolation began creating all sorts of emotions inside of me. I remember going to the mall in the middle of the day and buying myself a new top just so I'd feel good about myself. How awful. I didn't need it (sometimes I couldn't even afford it), but I felt so out of touch with everything that I was used to doing in God's Work… I wanted to be a part of it, but I couldn't, and sometimes I felt as if I was being punished.

And then I took it out on my son Filipe. Yes, the poor little guy, who had nothing to do with any of it, got an earful of my ongoing complaints about how much I wished I could be where all the action was, but couldn't because of him. I wasn't there for him whole-heartedly, and he knew it.

I started having many problems with Filipe. I had school complaints about him every single day. The other mothers would stand back and look at me with disgust; no matter how much I talked to Filipe, how much I spent time with him, he'd always be silly in school and give me embarrassing awkward

I began being the last one to hear about things that happened, and that feeling of isolation began creating all sorts of emotions inside of me.

The /woman

moments at the teacher's desk. I guess he was taking it out on others too…

I felt like the worst mother in the world. I was home all the time but it felt as though I wasn't. I neglected it. I knew that God wanted me to stay home and take care of my son, and I obeyed, but not wholeheartedly. I wanted to be somewhere else. I wanted to be where I had vowed I'd be for the rest of my life: on the altar[3].

Life became a routine for me those days, and I got bored. I began having many problems in my marriage as a result of my dissatisfaction with the way my life had turned out to be. While my husband was enjoying working for God, I wasn't enjoying working at home at all.

But I remember when that boredom stopped. I remember like it was yesterday. I stopped waiting for things to change for me; I stopped waiting for my son to get better and for

> Life became a routine for me those days, and I got bored. I began having many problems in my marriage…

[3] When you give all your life to serve as a pastor or pastor's wife, no future plans for yourself, no time-off, just work to save souls for as long as you live.

my husband to start including me in the picture. I began making things happen for myself.

First, I began praying that God would show me how I could serve Him where I was. I knew that He wanted me there, but how could I be there if I didn't feel good there? How could I add anything to my family if I felt frustrated all the time? I was honest with God: "I know this is Your will; I know You want me home taking care of Filipe, but I'm not happy here. I feel far from the Work that I have dedicated my life to. Help me serve You here, at home, and still be part of Your Work, Lord. I wasn't called to be home."

And so He answered me.

I began reaching out to others from home. I began writing articles, counseling people through letters and emails. I started thinking of new ideas on how to do more for God. And you know what happens when you start focusing on an idea? New ideas start to grow from the first ones.

I became a weekly columnist for the church's magazine, which as a result, got me to reach women I had never spoken to in church. Women started being helped through my columns, which soon be-

The woman

came international. Just a few years later, the book "Better Than a New Pair of Shoes" was the result of it all.

My columns were successful, and I started to feel confident enough to do more from home; so I began making radio programs and podcasts. Suddenly, my time at home felt like real work. I was home all the time, homeschooling my son, and helping my husband in church at the same time.

I felt useful – and you know how awesome that feels. The more you give to others, the more you receive from God. And the beauty of it all is that, once you begin being creative, you never stop. You enjoy it; it feels productive, alive, fun, and exciting.

AGING WITH NO CHILDREN

In 2 Kings 4:8-17, we read about a rich woman from Shunem, whom the Bible calls a Shunammite, who lived an uneventful life. She had been married for a number of years but had no children of her own, so you can imagine how that must have felt for a woman in those days when children were proof that God was pleased with you. She was an auntie to many, but not a mother. It must have been difficult for her, though the Bible doesn't go into that detail.

> *One day Elisha went to Shunem. And a well-to-do woman was there, who urged him to stay for a meal. So whenever he came by, he stopped there to eat. She said to her husband, "I know that this man who often comes our way is a holy man of God. Let's make a small room on the roof and put in it a bed and a table, a chair and a lamp for him. Then he can stay there whenever he comes to us.*

(2 Kings 4:8-10 NIV)

How beautiful it is to see a woman come up with bright ideas such as these. I don't think her husband would have ever thought of this. Not because he didn't care, but because it's really a "woman thing"... we like to put ourselves in other people's shoes. She

The more you give to others, the more you receive from God. ...once you begin being creative, you never stop.

The woman

must have felt bad for Elisha, traveling all the time, not having a family of his own, and still always ready to help others in service to God.

She got creative. She thought of making a room on the roof, which means there was no spare room at that time. Once you get creative, things pop into your head. She even thought of a chair and a lamp for him. She could see him taking his time in her house, staying a few more days than usual, resting, and having a cozy place to stay.

One day when Elisha came, he went up to his room and lay down there. He said to his servant Gehazi, "Call the Shunammite."

So he called her, and she stood before him. Elisha said to him, "Tell her, 'You have gone to all this trouble for us. Now what can be done for you? Can we speak on your behalf to the king or the commander of the army?'" She replied, "I have a home among my own people."

"What can be done for her?" Elisha asked. Gehazi

Once you get creative, things pop into your head.

said, "Well, she has no son and her husband is old." Then Elisha said, "Call her." So he called her, and she stood in the doorway. "About this time next year," Elisha said, "you will hold a son in your arms."

> *"No, my lord," she objected. "Don't mislead your servant, O man of God!" But the woman became pregnant, and the next year about that same time she gave birth to a son, just as Elisha had told her.*

(2 Kings 4:11-17 NIV)

That's where being creative gets you... it reawakens dreams you may even have given up on. It gives wings to your abilities, causing you to achieve things you never thought you could. This woman never asked for a child of her own, she never asked for anything in return, but her attitude towards Elisha meant a lot to him.

Sometimes, when you're being creative, you have no idea of the magnitude of that new project. I certainly never thought that starting a little column would take me to where I am today.

That extra room on the roof she made for Elisha was probably used later on for her newborn son.

The woman

Who would have thought that her simple act of creative kindness was actually creating a new member of her family?

I've heard women say they're not creative, and though I know they actually believe that about themselves, I also know it's not true. Anyone can be creative because it's a talent God gave to everyone. We come with it already installed in our brain – it's there for the taking!

In what area of your life can you become more creative?

How can you become more aware of opportunities around you?

My Notes

She's honorable

Strength and honor are her clothing; she shall rejoice in time to come.

(Proverbs 31:25)

 ccording to most dictionaries, honor means the following and more:

    1. honesty, fairness, or integrity in one's beliefs and actions

    2. a source of credit or distinction

    3. high respect, as for worth, merit, or rank

    4. such respect manifested

    5. high public esteem, fame, glory

Honor is about one's reputation and one's true character. One may buy or even

demand respect from others, but only those who truly deserve it, get it.

The V-Woman deserves honor, and it's not because she's better than anyone or because she's super woman, but because her life is a proof of that. She doesn't need to ask for the honor she's due.

More often than not, we want to prove to others that we're honorable, when, in fact, we can't ever prove that to anyone. It's one of the few things in life that cannot be manipulated. If you're a respectful person, you don't need to tell anyone that; you don't need to highlight it. People can tell by the smallest things you do.

A respectful woman is always for what's right. There's no debate about whether or not she'll tell the truth or be honest. Her character is such that lies are not a part of her life. She always tells the truth and she always honors her word. If she's saying

> If you're a respectful person, you don't need to tell anyone that; you don't need to highlight it.

something, you can count on her that she really means it and that she'll fulfill it.

People may not like her for a number of reasons (you know how people don't really need good reasons for that), but deep inside, they respect her in secret.

It's obvious that an honorable woman is not perfect, but because of her honorable character, she sometimes looks perfect. She just knows how to handle her mistakes. Anyone who knows how to turn a mistake into a blessing is worth our respect. It's like falling from a high place and landing on both feet every time.

This verse also shows how honor comes right after strength. You can't overcome anything if you don't have some sort of strength; and if you start thinking of all the people you know whom you find honorable, you'll also find this common trait: they're strong.

This is another kind of strength; it's related to honor. "Before destruction the heart of a man is haughty, and before honor is humility" (Proverbs 18:12).

This proverb sums up honor quite well and it describes the often disregarded strength that brings one honor. In order for one to be respected and honored, one needs to be humble. Humble to change, humble to

The /woman

do what's right, humble to recognize one's mistakes, and even humble to use faith as it is.

This is definitely not the kind of humbleness that is complacent with problems as they come. You're not honored when you're being beaten to death by poverty, diseases, or other insufferable problems.

You're humble when you're open to change, when your ego is not the most important thing in the world to you, when you don't have to have the last word in a disagreement, or when you don't have to prove a point. Humbleness is a strength most people lack; that's why only few have what follows it – honor.

The V-Woman had both strength and honor; in other words, humbleness and reputation. Both will always walk together. You can't be humble and not have a good reputation, and you can't have a good reputation and not be humble. The proud may be respected for what they do, but never for who they are.

If you've built a reputation on your career success, or perhaps, on the family that you've raised, and you're respected for it, here's a warning: your reputation is built upon things that you've conquered. If you lose those things, your reputation is at risk.

But if you're humble, you see things that others don't; you have guidance from above. So even when you lose the very things you've achieved, you don't feel like it's the end of the world for you. Your spirit is strong enough to help you achieve the same again.

You don't fall into depression; you don't feel like giving up, you don't go wild, tearing down the things that are still left standing. A lot of people who relied on others have gone down this road. You need to have a strong core.

The V-Woman had a strong core; she was strong and honorable. Anything that could possibly happen to her would not be enough to tear her apart. When you meet people as strong as that, you immediately and automatically respect them. You admire their strength, especially because of what they've gone through. They inspire you to be better; to go until the end.

No wonder the V-Woman can rejoice in time

You can't be humble and not have a good reputation, and you can't have a good reputation and not be humble.

to come. If you know that you have what it takes to go through whatever happens, you also feel secure with yourself. You're not afraid of the future and you run towards it with all that you've got, because you have this assurance inside of you. You're strong enough.

DISCRETION COMES WITH IT

Her honorable character is also a result of her own discretion. The Bible talks about discretion in a very interesting and clear way. Picture a pig playing in the mud with a diamond ring in its nose. Hard to visualize, isn't it? But that is how the Bible describes a woman who lacks discretion (read Proverbs 11:22). Harsh, but very true.

Discretion means the quality of behaving or speaking in such a way as to avoid causing offence or revealing private information; in other words, it is

> Discretion means the quality of behaving or speaking in such a way as to avoid causing offence or revealing private information...

the ability to discern what is and what is not appropriate to say or do.

Many women don't realize how important discretion is in determining their reputation before others. They try to show much goodness and gentleness towards others, but when it comes to being discreet, they're clueless.

Women who easily gossip about others, criticize others, talk about private matters with people who are not involved, and are sarcastic and rude to others, are often at the wrong place, at the wrong time, and with the wrong people. No matter how beautiful they look or how intelligent they are, lack of discretion will tear down their reputation down.

You're also lacking discretion when you're yelling at others. Think of a mother you've seen do this to her child in public; now, remind yourself how you felt towards her.

Beauty becomes futile when discretion does not accompany it. If there's no discretion, there's no beauty — let alone respect! If beauty, which is seen, is overshadowed by lack of indiscretion, imagine respect and honor...

Discretion also means avoiding trouble. Let's go over some examples and think of how you can turn them around so that you start your discretion process and, consequently, start being respected.

1. **Gossiping or criticizing others** – this indicates that you most probably have few friends, and the friends you have most probably do not trust you. When someone gossips with you, they will certainly gossip about you. If you want your friends to respect you, stop doing what they do when it comes to gossiping. Make it clear to them that you don't tolerate such a thing.

2. **Sharing private matters with others** – this means that you cannot be trusted with any important confidential information, and that your family is often the victim of your unnecessary comments and conversations. Why not avoid it altogether if you know you won't be able to keep it a secret? Tell your friend you can't really keep a secret, so you prefer not to hear it. And if you do feel like sharing some private information about your loved ones with others, ask yourself this question: How would I feel if they did that to me? The answer to that question will already be enough to help you.

3. Inappropriate joke — this simply makes you look like a fool, and fools are not pleasant people to be around. Have you ever met a joker who was also respected? Unheard of.

4. Yelling and speaking loudly — this shows that you're throwing all your femininity down the drain and that you're very hard to deal with. If you have to call out to someone who's far away from you, try to get closer or ask someone else to call him or her for you. It's hard to respect someone who can't respect others… very hard.

5. Flirting with men — this may seem naïve at first, but women who like doing this are showing quite the contrary. You're not understood when you're flirting; you're simply giving others an extra reason to criticize you. It's never honorable to witness a woman flirt because she often comes across as easy and unattached. Men often take advantage of such.

> Beauty becomes futile when discretion does not accompany it. If there's no discretion, there's no beauty...

6. Being rude to your loved ones – this also suggests that you'll be even ruder to those who are not your loved ones. Can you ever respect a daughter who disrespects her own mother? Can you ever respect a wife who disrespects her own husband? Again... very hard.

7. Indiscretion in the way you dress – when you're revealing too much, you're also saying you're not that special underneath your clothes; anybody can have a peek or some kind of preview. A respectful woman respects herself first, and her body is sacred, no matter what fashion dictates.

Being honorable is about having common sense too. You're not a follower of crowds; you're smart enough to see where you're going and what you're doing.

UNHAPPILY MARRIED

It's never honorable to witness a woman flirt because she often comes across as easy and unattached.

Abigail "was a woman of good understanding and beautiful appearance." Her story in 1 Samuel 25 begins when her husband, Nabal, turns away from helping David and his men. All that was needed from Nabal was to be hospitable and help them in their journey ahead. David's good reputation was known all over Israel at this time even though he wasn't officially a king yet. Nevertheless, Nabal, in his pride, not only turns his hand away, but also humiliates David by saying:

> *Who is David, and who is the son of Jesse? There are many servants nowadays who break away each one from his master. Shall I then take my bread and my water and my meat that I have killed for my shearers, and give it to men when I do not know where they are from?*

(1 Samuel 25:10,11)

Have you met people who will make a big deal out of small favors asked? How did they come across to you and those who witnessed the "dramatic scene"? Quite sad… even though they may have had a point, they lost it there and then just by the way they handled the situation. Nabal may not have met David before, but he certainly didn't need to turn up his nose at him this way. In fact, David and his men even helped to protect the land

during their stay in Nabal's lands; the least Nabal could have done was to have thanked them for their peaceful stay and protection provided towards his workers.

As soon as the messengers passed on the disdainful message to David, he gathered 400 men and went his way to fight Nabal. This distressing news about what was about to happen to her husband came to Abigail's knowledge, and she didn't waste any time.

> *Then Abigail made haste and took two hundred loaves of bread, two skins of wine, five sheep already dressed, five seahs of roasted grain, one hundred clusters of raisins, and two hundred cakes of figs, and loaded them on donkeys. And she said to her servants, "Go on before me; see, I am coming after you." But she did not tell her husband Nabal. So it was, as she rode on the donkey, that she went down under cover of the hill; and there were David and his men, coming down toward her, and she met them.*

(1 Samuel 25:18-20)

The woman really went out of her way to make up for her husband's thoughtless attitude. She prepared a real feast for David and his men. But the beauty of it is that she did what most of us would probably dare not do. First she recognized her husband's mistakes.

EThis in itself is one of the hardest things for a wife to do. She'll often point out his mistakes to his face, but she'll rarely recognize his mistakes before others. I sometimes witness this in the ministry. A pastor is rebuked for something he has done, and his wife, instead of recognizing why her husband needs to change and helping him do that, takes his side just because he's her husband. God never meant for us wives to push our husbands down further into the abyss when they're falling. We're supposed to be our husband's helpmate, right arm, and partner; to do what it takes to help him — even what might be misunderstood as taking the other side.

Now when Abigail saw David, she dismounted quickly from the donkey, fell on her face

God never meant for us wives to push our husbands down further into the abyss when they're falling.

The *W*woman

before David, and bowed down to the ground. So she fell at his feet and said: "On me, my lord, on me let this iniquity be! And please let your maidservant speak in your ears, and hear the words of your maidservant.

Please, let not my lord regard this scoundrel Nabal. For as his name is, so is he: Nabal is his name, and folly is with him! But I, your maidservant, did not see the young men of my lord whom you sent. Now therefore, my lord, as the LORD lives and as your soul lives, since the LORD has held you back from coming to bloodshed and from avenging yourself with your own hand, now then, let your enemies and those who seek harm for my lord be as Nabal.

We're supposed to be our husband's helpmate, right arm, and partner; to do what it takes to help him...

And now this present which your maidservant has brought to my lord, let it be given to the young men who follow my lord. Please forgive the trespass of your maidservant. For the LORD will certainly make for my lord an enduring house, because my lord fights the battles of the LORD, and evil is not found in you throughout your days. Yet a man has risen to pursue you and seek your life, but the life of my lord shall be bound in the bundle of the living with the LORD your God; and the lives of your enemies He shall sling out, as from the pocket of a sling.

And it shall come to pass, when the LORD has done for my lord according to all the good that He has spoken concerning you, and has appointed you ruler over Israel, that this will be no grief to you, nor offense of heart to my lord, either that you have shed blood without cause, or that my lord has avenged himself. But when the LORD has dealt well with my lord, then remember your maidservant."

(1 Samuel 25:23-31)

Again, Abigail went out of her way to beg David for mercy on behalf of her husband and her household. She even goes on to say that it's also her fault as she wasn't around when David's messengers showed up in her house. How respectable of her! She recognized her husband's faults and hers, and humbly apologized for them before David.

Honorable women don't have a problem in apologizing. Their humbleness is their very essence. Have you noticed that whenever someone is humble enough to apologize, you're immediately in awe of it? We admire people who can come to terms with their mistakes and we despise it whenever people get too defensive about their mistakes.

> *Blessed is the LORD God of Israel, who sent you this day to meet me! And blessed is your advice and blessed are you [...] Go up in peace to your house. See, I have heeded your voice and respected your person."*

(1 Samuel 25:32,33,35)

Abigail's humbleness, servitude, and promptness to apologize on her household's behalf won David's respect to the point where he even asked her to marry him when her husband died some time later, to which she gladly answered: "Here is your maidservant, a servant to wash the feet of the servants of my lord" (1 Samuel 25:41).

What an impression she made on David. What an honorable woman she was. And when you think of it, she didn't do much. She was simply strong enough to be humble.

Describe how you can be honorable towards your family and co-workers.

Think of your next step to apply what you answered above.

Honorable women don't have a problem in apologizing. Their humbleness is their very essence.

The V woman

My Notes

_____

_____

_____

_____

_____

_____

_____

_____

_____

_____

_____

_____

_____

_____

_____

_____

_____

_____

_____

She's sweet

*She opens her mouth with wisdom, and
on her tongue is the law of kindness.*

(Proverbs 31:26)

Have you ever met someone who's extremely smart, has all the right answers, and knows how to handle practically anything in life, but at the same time makes you feel uncomfortable just by being around?

There are plenty of wise female wizards out there. They always have a lecture to give and the minute you say something incorrect (which often happens to those of us who are just not as "high up" as they are), they look down on you. They're too good for us. They say they're human and full of mistakes, but I don't think they mean it one bit.

The /woman

The V-Woman is wise, but her wisdom does not make anyone feel bad because she's kind too. The verse above shows us something we don't always think about: wisdom has a lot to do with speaking and kindness. I always thought that in order to be wise, one would know what to do, how to behave, and how to handle life. But according to this verse, it's the way we speak.

The Bible says that "out of the abundance of the heart his mouth speaks" (Luke 6:45). This brings us to the conclusion that all the wisdom one has, comes out of one's mouth, and not necessarily through one's attitudes. This doesn't mean that a person will behave badly, but that the first point of contact for a woman's wisdom is through her words.

The V-Woman speaks wisely, and so she speaks kindly; she's sweet. Now let's turn this sentence around: The NON-V-Woman speaks foolishly, and so she speaks unkindly; she's bitter.

The V-Woman is wise, but her wisdom does not make anyone feel bad because she's kind too.

Sad people are always looking at others in a sad way. They're so frustrated with their own lives that the only way to make them feel better is to look at others, who seem to be doing fine, and criticize, hate, and put them down. Everything can be a reason for criticism in the eyes of those who are unhappy with themselves.

When a mother screams at her child after tripping up on a toy in the middle of the living room... when a wife pulls a face at her husband because he doesn't help out with the household chores... when a young woman rolls her eyes when a friend calls at an inconvenient time... She wishes that she could turn a blind eye to some of these things, she wishes to at least know how to handle these small insignificant blocks, but she can't; she has tried before and failed.

So how do you combat this? It's simple but not easy. It's completely doable; no need for manuals, you just have to do the opposite of what you feel like doing. If the shoes in the middle of the living room floor are screaming for you to lose your temper, don't give them the satisfaction. Simply pick them up and put them in their place.

So simple isn't it? This is how you can deal with everything that comes your way – dealing with things in a positive way, leaving all the bitterness aside.

You see, when you deal with things in a negative way, you attract negative reaction. For instance, the child will react by rolling his eyes and saying something to hurt you back, or the husband will feel that his manhood is threatened by your disrespect and walk out the door... Sow negative seeds, reap negative fruits.

The minute you speak a little louder, the other person is bound to speak louder than you. Give someone a reason to be angry with you, and he or she will no longer focus on his or her mistake, where it all actually began, but rather on your anger.

Be sweet about it. Instead of returning like for like to the person who hurt you, put it all aside and leave it at that. You don't always have to win an argument. You don't always have to let others know what they've done wrong. You don't always have to point out people's shortcomings. And you could certainly do without the nagging, after all, isn't it more than proven now that the more you nag, the less you're heard?

Proverbs 19:13 illustrates it very nicely: "And the contentions of a wife are a continual dripping."

If you have ever been annoyed by a leaky tap, then you have some idea of how annoying a nagging mother is to a child when she nags him or her about school, for example; or how a husband feels when his wife is nagging him the minute he arrives home from work about the unpaid bills, or the fact that she's the only one doing anything at home, and so on.

This doesn't mean she doesn't have a good reason to nag; it just means that she's like that continual dripping. No one wants to listens to her; no one wants to pay attention to her needs. Her family just makes it a point to avoid home altogether...

I used to be a nag and I know that we don't really mean to be one. We want to get things done and since we're not heard the first time we speak, we start all over again on each subject until someone actually listens to us. But unfortunately, during this process, we lose our sweetness and become this totally boring wife or mother to come home to.

My husband worked hard every day, and the little time left for me,

> The minute you speak a little louder, the other person is bound to speak louder than you.

he'd take to sleep, which annoyed me very much. I wanted to go out, discover, and watch movies... and he wanted to rest. We had the same dilemma every week. I'd complain about it or sometimes use those below-the-belt comments we're experts at making, and he'd either give me the silent treatment or grudgingly take me out. I felt horrible either way and I didn't know how to express myself other than in those two ways.

This went on for quite some time until I realized I was wrong. It was hard to admit to my wrong behavior in trying to have some quality time with my husband... Don't we wives deserve that? But that wasn't the problem, that wasn't wrong; the problem was the nagging about it, the continual resistance to my husband's wishes.

> My husband worked hard every day, and the little time left for me, he'd take to sleep...

I started to take this matter to God and, in turn, He started to show me how to get what I wanted without the nagging. First,

I stopped nagging. Then I started doing the things my husband wanted to do and stayed home without the long face or usual complaints. And a few weeks later (yes, it took me only weeks!), my husband was trying to please me in return. He began taking the initiative and taking me out and enjoying it too.

I decided to be sweet and kind to my husband and that was enough for him to feel obliged to be sweet and kind to me too

PASSIONATE ABOUT BELONGING

The book of Song of Songs in the Bible talks about the love story of the Shulamite and her beloved. It portrays an intimate relationship between a man and his wife, a symbol of God and His Church. There's romance from beginning to end; one not having enough of the other, full of passion for one another – the kind of story that dreams are made of.

The Shulamite may be a fictional name, but she certainly shows the true behavior of a woman who's got it all: sweetness, humbleness, honor, creativity, beauty, and everything else we've covered about the V-Woman. She's delightful and fun; and I'd like to en-

courage you to read about her in some of the verses from The Message Bible version I've picked below.

If this is the woman God wanted to use to represent His Church, or to represent all women, these verses will give you a pretty good idea about how sweet and lovely she was and how we have to be:

> *Kiss me — full on the mouth! Yes! For your love is better than wine.*

> (Song of Songs 1:2)

Here's a woman who appreciates her husband's kisses and finds his love better than any other pleasure out there.

> *Don't look down on me because I'm dark, darkened by the sun's harsh rays. My brothers ridiculed me and sent me to work in the fields. They made me care for the face of the earth, but I had no time to care for my own face.*

> (Song of Songs 1:6)

She worked hard, just like most working moms nowadays; but that wasn't a reason to be bitter, nor to let her love be burdened by it.

And you, my dear lover — you're so handsome! And the bed we share is like a forest glen.

(Song of Songs 1:16)

She found her husband attractive and enjoyed their time in bed.

My lover stands above the young men in town. All I want is to sit in his shade, to taste and savor his delicious love. He took me home with him for a festive meal, but his eyes feasted on me!

(Song of Songs 2:3,4)

The Shulamite admired her husband and no one compared to him. And just like she made him feel special, he made her feel special too.

The Shulamite may be a fictional name, but she certainly shows the true behavior of a woman who's got it all...

 The woman

My lover is mine, and I am his.

(Song of Songs 2:16)

Isn't this unheard of these days – to belong to a man? But what if you belong to a man that also belongs to you? What if you've found the one for you? The Shulamite had found him and she rejoiced in every minute of her time with him.

I threw my arms around him and held him tight, wouldn't let him go until I had him home again, safe at home beside the fire.

(Song of Songs 3:4)

His words are kisses, his kisses words. Everything about him delights me, thrills me through and through! That's lover, that's my man.

(Song of Songs 5:16)

I am my lover's. I'm all he wants. I'm all the world to him!

(Song of Songs 7:9)

Isn't this
unheard of
these days – to
belong to a man?

Hang my locket around your neck, wear my ring on your finger. Love is invincible facing danger and death. Passion laughs at the terrors of hell. The fire of love stops at nothing – it sweeps everything before it.

(Song of Songs 8:6)

She showed him how much she loved him in simple gestures that are so important and needed in any relationship: hugging, kissing, and words of love and appreciation. Only the sweet have those in stock!

You don't need to write a poem to a friend or a loved one to exhale this kind of "perfume" wherever you go; sometimes all it takes is doing something you haven't yet done. When was the last time you showed some kind of appreciation towards someone you love?

We waste so much time trying to get things in place that we forget why we want these things in place in the first place. We take care of our home because it's our home and our family lives there. It's for them to feel at home, and to feel good coming home at the end of the day. If we nag and we're bitter, we'll defeat the purpose of what we were trying to achieve in the first place.

How often do marriages grow cold because the wife gets too busy with the children's school and school clubs, and completely ignores the lover who gave her those children?

Being sweet makes us feel good about ourselves. A compliment out of the blue can literally change the whole atmosphere at home. Many times when I feel my teenage son is distant from me, I make it a point to compliment him on something he has done, and when he hasn't done anything, I ask him to do something I know he enjoys and does well, like cooking, just so I can tell him how delicious it was... it works every time.

What are some sweet attitudes you can start putting into practice with those you love?

How's wisdom related to being kind?

My Notes

She's busy

She watches over the ways of her household, and does not eat the bread of idleness.

(Proverbs 31:27)

Idleness is one of today's worst characteristics among young women. How often do you hear them say "I'm tired" in a day? They do what they do because they have to do it. If they could, they'd stop going to school and just hang out either shut in their room with a computer in hand or with friends at the mall. They add nothing to society except high telephone bills to be paid.

I remember my younger years and I know how hard it can be to go to school every day, to come home and just feel like sitting in front of a TV and drink in whatever we're offered. I know what it's like to go to bed and have a hard time getting to

The/woman

sleep because of all the dreams you wish could be fulfilled one day. I know that little world we create for ourselves, and how it helps us feel protected and manage the loneliness; how a pet can truly be our best friend and a teddy bear our way of taking out all the stress.

Idleness does this to us. The idler we are, the less productive, and the more futile our thoughts are. Take daydreaming for example.

Daydreams come and go throughout the day; you may be at work or in school, driving or walking on the streets, or simply lying in bed. They're like the waves of the sea, non-stop, taking you far away from where you were in the first place. Suddenly, your things left on shore are so far away from you that anyone can simply steal your belongings right in front of your eyes. That's what daydreams do to us. They take us to places that will never exist or to events that will never happen, while in the real world, we lose sight of what is really going on in our lives.

The idler we are, the less productive, and the more futile our thoughts are.

I used to daydream a lot and I know exactly how these fake images can make a girl feel, especially if she's a loner and feels inferior to other girl. In your dreams, the real you sits in the audience and the fake you takes center stage. And there she is in the spotlight. She's special, known, popular, admired by everyone, wanted by everyone, and everything anyone would ever want to be. Problem is, the minute you're back to your senses, you find yourself so far away from what you wanted to be that you can't help but feel frustrated with yourself, as if you're never going to be good enough.

Then, as if that's not enough for your already below-average confidence level, your studies or work also begins to be affected. Consequently, you're not doing as well as everyone else around you and you are at risk of losing out or simply being known as "the not so bright one".

Surely, the big deal should be about what's real. Reality is what matters and if that is not working so well for you, work at it, strive to get it back or simply do better at it. Everyone can be who they want to be, but few actually realize this in time; the rest day dream their life away as if they had all the time in the world to come back down to earth some day.

When that "some day" comes along, it could be too late, you could be too old, or made so many wrong decisions in the past that now you can't afford to pursue your real dreams.

Life will not wait for you to wake up. It'll go on and precious time will be wasted – there's no doubt about that. The only way to avoid this nonsense is to get busy.

Don't let your mind rest. Focus on something and when that's finished, focus on something else, until you're too tired to think and you simply go to sleep. You'll be doing yourself a big favor, getting better at what you do, applying yourself to new things, creating new talents and new skills, and overall making reality a much better dream to have.

Anyone can be busy and being busy alone will not necessarily make you a V-Woman. Make sure you're busy first with things that only you can do. If you have time for anything else, then by all means, add more.

Here's a list of things ONLY YOU can do for yourself:

• **Take care of your health** – to eat right, exercise, and take good care of your body are usually the last things on our to-do lists; change that pattern, make it number one. After all, if you're sick, how will you ever get to the remaining items on that list?

• **Take care of your spiritual life** – praying, reading the Bible, attending church at least twice a week, and keeping your heart free from grudges and all kinds of bad things that can easily be passed on to the next day, week, month, year, until it's too late to do anything about it... People fall into sin all the time for this reason. Be smarter than that.

• **Give of yourself** – nobody can do it for you. If you keep on waiting to receive in order to give to others, you might as well lie down and wait to die. Always ask yourself this question: How can I give more of myself today? This way, you'll always be giving and you'll always be receiving. It's a great way to live!

• **Be yourself** – only you can do that, so why keep on trying to be someone else? Do people buy the same pair of shoes twice?

Don't let your mind rest. Focus on something and when that's finished, focus on something else...

No way! I hate replicas, I hate knowing that I don't have the real thing… it's either the original or nothing.

• **Be responsible** – whatever post you've been given in life, do it well. If you're a mother, daughter, employee, wife, homemaker, or student, know this: only you can do those well. So why waste time?

Another very good reason for you to be busy is because of what comes along with idleness: it's one of the main reasons why you're constantly bombarded by evil thoughts. If your mind is idle, it'll attract all the dust this world has. Isn't that how empty homes can sometimes even look scary? Cobwebs everywhere, dust, and strange looking bugs are just a few of the things you can find. Nobody lives there but instead of remaining clean as it had been left, it attracts dirt and all sorts.

If you keep on waiting to receive in order to give to others, you might as well lie down and wait to die.

That's how the mind operates too. If you don't get into the habit of learning new things or thinking of solutions to different challenges, it's empty and plain; and just like a muscle that you never use, it begins to feel useless, attracting all kinds of worthless ideas into it.

The V-Woman is constantly watching for ways to improve herself and her family. She doesn't stop at one success. There's no TIME OUT, because that often really means TIME WASTED.

Idle people are easily distracted from their goals too. They'll tell you how much they want to change one day, and then the next day they'll show you how much they don't care to do so. They find it hard to focus on good things because they're often idle, too lazy to think, too lazy to help themselves.

It's very sad because their potential is wasted — and usually during the best time of their life, when they're young and full of energy. By the time they come to their senses, they're usually too old to do many of the things they wish to do, and regret takes over.

"If only I had done it differently when I was growing up," they think. What's the use of thinking that way now? If you've wasted a lot of your past, change things from now on, starting with getting yourself busy. Don't let idleness get the better of you.

I like to be busy to the point of not having time to feel sad or to entertain feelings, and it usually works for me. In fact, I make fewer mistakes when I'm busy. The minute I miss someone and the memories start surfacing, I quickly disregard them, as if I were numb to them. It's not that I don't feel them; I decide to disregard them and I get busy instead. I do the same when I'm sad.

I began this habit a few years ago, when I was diagnosed with a very bad cat allergy. At the time, I had a beautiful 2-year-old Ragdoll cat. His name was Josh and he had deep blue eyes, was extremely intelligent, caring, and good tempered. I had no say on the matter; as soon as I got back home from the doctor's office, the cat was gone. My husband loved that cat, but he loved me more; and so, he arranged everything so that I wouldn't even say goodbye to Josh.

My heart wanted to cry and beg for a chance to keep the cat, even if that meant taking extra medication, but my head knew I couldn't have the cat and there was nothing anybody could do about it. My heart was broken, but I decided to not feel it… I remember how I made it a point to never talk about that cat again. Every time people brought up the subject, I'd politely tell them, "I don't want to talk about that."

And since it worked in that silly instance, I concluded it must also work for other more important issues in my life. That's when I began getting myself busy, too busy to notice any feeling or emotion that would often drag me down for days.

DOING A MAN'S JOB

Deborah was an extraordinary woman who had a very busy life. You can read her story in Judges 4 and 5. She was a prophetess and a judge, something unusual in those days, when married women were mostly housewives. The people of Israel would often come to her for advice and be to get justice, which already says a lot about the woman.

Few people actually trust others to the point of letting them judge their case and give them advice. We are very suspicious of one another; it's a human

I like to be busy to the point of not having time to feel sad or to entertain feelings, and it usually works for me.

trait. There's always that fear that someone is taking advantage of us and we need to defend and protect ourselves at all costs – even if that means suffering alone.

Deborah wasn't only trusted to be the judge and prophetess in Israel, but she was also the one everyone looked up to. When the time came for Israel to go to war, they only wanted to go if she'd go with them. A woman had to go to war in order for the entire army to go... What an extraordinary woman!

If you don't know her story well, you're probably thinking she was one of these single independent successful career women. Well, you're wrong. Deborah was also a housewife and she served Israel out of love and faith towards God. She didn't do this because of the status or the power she'd get out of it; so much so that when she was requested to join Barak, Naphtali's tribe leader, during the war, she said:

Few people actually trust others to the point of letting them judge their case and give them advice.

I will surely go with you; nevertheless there will be no glory for you in the journey you are taking, for the LORD will sell Sisera into the hand of a woman.

(Judges 4:9)

It's not that she wanted to turn her nose up at his request, but she wanted to advise him that people would know that she was the reason they all went to war and they'd credit her for their victory.

You wouldn't think that a housewife and a mother could also be a prophetess, a judge, and now a soldier! There's no doubt about the fact that Deborah was a busy woman, and also that she was good at what she did – otherwise, people wouldn't have listened to her. One thing is to be busy and be a terrible housewife and mother; another thing is to be busy and be good at all the things that make you busy. This makes people respect you, because they see you practice what you preach.

Israel had peace during Deborah's time not because she was perfect, but because she got herself busy with things that mattered. They didn't have a judge or a ruler at the time; she gladly took the post. They didn't have a proper war hero to follow to war;

she gladly took the post. And in all her busy time, you see the intentions of her heart to serve God above all.

Perhaps that's where the difference in her was. She was busy for God. When you're busy for God, you're too busy to make mistakes.

What would you say has led you to idleness?

What can you do to avoid it altogether and start focusing more on getting yourself busy with worthy causes?

My Notes

She's praised

Her children rise up and call her blessed;
her husband also, and he praises her:
Many daughters have done well, but you
excel them all.

(Proverbs 31:28,29)

*Y*ou don't become a V-Woman so you can be compared to others. You don't become a V-Woman so you can be better than others. You become a V-Woman because it's THE RIGHT THING TO DO. Why not? Why wouldn't you be a better woman, wife, daughter, mother, homemaker, friend, and sister?

I was surprised to read a comment left for me on one of my blog posts: "Sometimes everyone feels the same. One thing I know for sure, time goes fast and we always regret not doing things we like. Don't look

around you. Don't make yourself a role model. Enjoy your life. You're beautiful! Inside and out."

She was probably just trying to be nice, as if to say, it's okay if you make mistakes, don't be too tough on yourself. Quite a nice thing to say to someone, isn't it? For a while, I even accepted it. But then I thought, "Who said I'm trying to be a role model? All I want is to be better; and with that, glorify my Lord."

Movies have this same message. You don't have to be the best; just be yourself. But I ask, why not? Why can't we be the best? Why do we have to be average, mediocre women? I think, deep down, every woman wants to be better and wishes she'd be a role model to someone someday.

Some women have a gift for playing "THE VICTIM". They're always the victim of whatever bad situation they go through.

The verse above can actually come true for you and me, and do you know why? Because by now, we know how to be a V-Woman! People who know you won't be able to help but praise you for being so different from most women out there. As with anything in life, whenever one is different, one is noticed.

The problem is the usual female mentality we all have. It's always the same, whenever there's a problem with someone, instead of us looking at ourselves and working on that, we point out other people's flaws: "My husband is the problem", "Nobody understands me", "My parents don't help me", "My boss hates me", or "God doesn't care about me".

Some women have a gift for playing "THE VICTIM". They're always the victim of whatever bad situation they go through. And while they're in that role, they miss the whole point. Did you know that we go through difficulties so we can change and do better next time, and that we make mistakes so we can learn? More often than not, it's not that we're being misunderstood — it's that we do not really understand.

The V-Woman is constantly changing and so she's constantly excelling. Her family praises her; and because she does the things that most women don't care about, she is the one everyone looks up to. And with

that, she praises God in the very unpopular way – the practical way.

We should also understand one thing about being praised: it's not something you can ask other people to do. I know a lot of women who are constantly complaining about their husbands not showing much appreciation for their hard work; and with that, they're constantly nagging them.

Men are constantly put off by women's nagging. They can't stand it and some of them will even avoid showing any kind of appreciation just so they can teach their wives a lesson. Unfortunately, women don't learn that way. The more they're indifferent to their wives, the more their wives nag.

One would think that by now, after many years of trying the same method, women would have learned that it doesn't work – but they haven't. And the sad thing about it is that no one is sharing that wisdom either. Grandmothers did it, mothers do it, and daughters will get married and do it too.

We're so modern and yet so undeveloped when it comes to handling our problems. It would be nice if we could remain undeveloped with those things that work the old-fashioned way, and not with those things that never really worked.

If you want to be praised, you've got to stop demanding to be praised. The V-Woman did everything the best way possible, to the point that she surprised even her own family.

One thing is to surprise people who don't know you that well. A lot of women can do that. But to surprise those who live under the same roof as you... that's totally virtuous! They're the ones who know you best, and if they can praise you, anybody can.

OPPRESSED AND HUMILIATED

Hannah was barren and married to a husband who was crazy about her, but who also had to maintain his status. So he was also married to Peninnah, who gave him children and became Hannah's worst rival. Not only was she the other

Men are constantly put off by women's nagging. They can't stand it...

The woman

woman in Elkanah's life, but was also the reason why being barren worsened the problem. The woman wouldn't leave Hannah alone. You can imagine Peninnah hating Hannah, after having been chosen by Elkanah not out of love, but just so he could have children.

Every day was the same thing for Hannah. The constant bad jokes, the never-ending loneliness and fear of what would happen to her after Elkanah was gone were always simmering under the surface. She was a sad woman and her husband saw that. He'd say "Hannah, why do you weep? Why do you not eat? And why is your heart grieved? Am I not better to you than ten sons?" (1 Samuel 1:8).

> You don't read that she complained about Peninnah; you don't read that she made a scene at the dinner table.

Of course he was the love of her life, but he'd never understand what it was like not to have a child of his own, because he had children with his other mean wife.

So Hannah arose after they had finished eating and drinking in Shiloh.

(1 Samuel 1:9)

You don't read that she complained about Peninnah; you don't read that she made a scene at the dinner table. You read about her respecting dinner time, even though she didn't feel like being there. First lesson: she was sad but she didn't have to make others miserable because of it.

Now Eli the priest was sitting on the seat by the doorpost of the tabernacle of the LORD. And she was in bitterness of soul, and prayed to the LORD and wept in anguish.

(1 Samuel 1:9,10)

Again, you don't read about Hannah going to her friends and crying on their shoulders about how unfair her life was. Hannah doesn't even mind Eli's presence at the temple; she goes straight to God.

First she prayed and when there were no more words to describe how she felt, she wept bitterly. It's the kind of crying that comes from deep within. Tissues can't dry those tears; it's too deep to be explained. Nobody understood how she felt, but God did.

> *Then she made a vow and said, "O*
> *LORD of hosts, if You will indeed look on*
> *the affliction of Your maidservant and*
> *remember me, and not forget Your maid-*
> *servant, but will give Your maidservant*
> *a male child, then I will give him to the*
> *LORD all the days of his life, and no ra-*
> *zor shall come upon his head."*

(1 Samuel 1:11)

Once she had that assurance that only God can give, that everything was going to be all right, she made a vow with Him – a vow that was practically saying she'd be returning God's blessing to Him. This amazing attitude of hers moved God's hands to perform a miracle in her life.

You see, she wasn't asking for a child for herself anymore; she was asking to be a mother to a child who served God. Her goals changed. She was no longer thinking only about herself, her mother's ego, or her competition with Peninnah. I'm sure she had asked God for a child many other times, but this was the time it was recorded in the Bible. This was the time she stopped thinking about herself and started thinking about God.

And God did change her life from that day on, starting that very minute of the vow. The Bible says "So the woman went her way and ate, and her face was no longer sad" (1 Samuel 1:18).

God helped her be happy, regardless of what she didn't have. With that new and different attitude, Hannah became a different woman altogether.

> *And Elkanah knew Hannah his wife,*
> *and the LORD remembered her.*

(1 Samuel 1:19)

Hannah was no longer bitter, and Elkanah must have noticed how attractive she now looked. A bitter woman is never attractive, no matter how much makeup she puts on, no matter how much weight she loses. Here's another misconception of the world...

If you're feeling down, go shopping or go for a total physical transformation, as if that's going to

Once she (Hannah) had that assurance that only God can give, that everything was going to be all right, she made a vow with Him...

really change the way you feel. You might like what you see in the mirror, but you'll still not like how you feel or how you make others feel.

Bitterness and nagging walk together. Women who nag are also bitter, and bitter women also nag. Instead of you getting what you want from others, you get them to avoid you altogether.

Hannah took all her bitterness to God that day; she emptied herself, and to top it off, she decided to do the right thing. She decided to give God the glory for the first time in her life. Now you can imagine God's reaction to that. Usually, no one ever cares about what God wants from them.

> *So it came to pass in the process of time that Hannah conceived and bore a son, and called his name Samuel, saying, "Because I have asked for him from the LORD."*
>
> (1 Samuel 1:20)

A bitter woman is never attractive, no matter how much makeup she puts on, no matter how much weight she loses.

She immediately gave her newborn son a name

that wouldn't ever let her forget her vow to God. And from then on, the new mother gave her best to prepare Samuel to serve God for the rest of his life. And when he was of the right age to go, she didn't think twice. She didn't ask God for an extension of her vow.

She didn't do it bitterly either. She simply "took him up with her, with three bulls, one ephah of flour, and a skin of wine, and brought him to the house of the LORD in Shiloh. And the child was young. Then they slaughtered a bull, and brought the child to Eli. And she said, 'O my lord! As your soul lives, my lord, I am the woman who stood by you here, praying to the LORD. For this child I prayed, and the LORD has granted me my petition which I asked of Him. Therefore I also have lent him to the LORD; as long as he lives he shall be lent to the LORD.' So they worshiped the LORD there" (1 Samuel 1:24-28).

As long as he lives, he shall be lent to the LORD. What a beautiful attitude! For a mother to do that, she must have really meant it, for she took him to the temple and never ever got him back. And God, seeing her faithfulness and sacrifice, honored her with more children of her own.

1 Samuel 2 starts with her beautiful prayer:

> *My heart rejoices in the LORD; my horn is exalted in the LORD. I smile at my enemies, because I rejoice in Your salvation. No one is holy like the LORD, for there is none besides You, nor is there any rock like our God. Talk no more so very proudly; let no arrogance come from your mouth, for the LORD is the God of knowledge; and by Him actions are weighed.*

> *The bows of the mighty men are broken, and those who stumbled are girded with strength. Those who were full have hired themselves out for bread, and the hungry have ceased to hunger. Even the barren has borne seven, and she who has many children has become feeble.*

> *The LORD kills and makes alive; He brings down to the grave and brings up. The LORD makes poor and makes rich; He brings low and lifts up. He raises the poor from the dust and lifts the beggar from the ash heap, to set them*

among princes and make them inherit the throne of glory. For the pillars of the earth are the LORD's, and He has set the world upon them. He will guard the feet of His saints, but the wicked shall be silent in darkness.

For by strength no man shall prevail. The adversaries of the LORD shall be broken in pieces; from heaven He will thunder against them. The LORD will judge the ends of the earth. He will give strength to His king, and exalt the horn of His anointed.

Many people prayed in Bible times, but few of those prayers were recorded. Hannah's prayer is one of the few. Why does God make it a point to include Hannah's prayer in His Word? If you read it slowly, you'll understand why. Here's a woman who gives God all the glory. She's not saying,

> And God, seeing her (Hannah) faithfulness and sacrifice, honored her with more children of her own.

"Because I decided to do this, I achieved my greatest dream," like many people often say. Because she decided to praise God entirely for her blessings, God also decided to praise her.

You can be praised by your family and friends, but to be praised by God Himself, that's way above simple praise! God honored Hannah's sacrifice. That's what He does. Every time we sacrifice to Him, every time we go without for His honor, He honors us above and beyond.

If Hannah's prayer was so important as to make it to the Scriptures, what do you think her husband, her family, and friends thought of her? I'm sure Peninnah lacked that "good old sense of humor" about Hannah from then on.

Before honor is humility.

(Proverbs 18:12)

> If Hannah's prayer was so important as to make it to the Scriptures, what do you think her husband, her family, and friends thought of her?

If you really want to be praised, don't demand it; simply follow Hannah's V-Woman trait.

What kind of honor have you been looking for?

What can you do differently from now on to attain it?

My Notes

_____

_____

_____

_____

_____

_____

_____

_____

_____

_____

_____

_____

_____

_____

_____

_____

_____

_____

_____

_____

She fears God

Charm is deceitful and beauty is passing, but a woman who fears the LORD, she shall be praised.

(Proverbs 31:30)

In my opinion, this is the main characteristic of the V-Woman. She fears God. Any woman can be a good mother, a good housewife, a good friend, a good employee, and good boss if she wants to. All she needs to do is give her best and be an easy learner to do better each passing year. Nevertheless, the Virtuous Woman was more than just good in all those areas, she was also godly, which led her to be excellent in all those things – so much so that you're reading one more book about this amazing woman of the Bible.

Just like computers crash for a number of technical reasons, we can also crash in

many areas of our lives when our relationship with God is not doing so well. Try to remember the last time you had a problem in your marriage or with a friend. How was your spiritual life then? You may say it was all right, but by that you probably mean "dormant" and not at all active.

When God is the center of our lives, we can hardly focus our attention elsewhere. It's not to say we won't have problems, but we will certainly react to them in a very different way. And that's where many Christian women have failed.

I met this beautiful Christian woman in one of our marriage courses, who came to us as a last resort for her marriage. She was devastated with the way her marriage was going, couldn't take it anymore, and was ready to give up on it. But she came, and along came her husband, who was also clueless as to how he'd make the marriage work after all they had been through.

They attended the course from beginning to

> When God is the center of our lives, we can hardly focus our attention elsewhere.

end, came for a few private counseling sessions, and eventually started attending the church on Sundays. He, who had been skeptical about God all his life, began opening up to the new faith and even began seeing things in a different light after a few weeks.

Soon they were giving their testimony to everyone of their friends. She had forgiven him, and he had learned how to be a husband; they were now on the same wavelength and looking forward to the years ahead in each other's arms.

But time passed by and things started happening in their personal lives. Lots of distractions and so they began coming less and less to the church. There was always something else happening, and their new faith began fading away like any muscle does after you stop working it.

Months later, when they had completely stopped coming to the church (here's a pattern I've noticed: the less you do something, the less you want to do it; the more you do something, the more you want to do it), they were back in the same situation they were when they first came to us – in a rut. Their marriage had nowhere to turn to. They both had the skills to work on it, but neither had the strength to do it anymore.

It's sad to see this happening over and over again… people just don't get it. It's not enough to know what you have to do in order to have a happy fulfilled life. It's not enough to have all the skills for it. You've got to have the one missing tool that cannot be learned or acquired, but built – a true relationship with God.

If you want to stop crashing in your marriage, at your workplace, among relatives or friends, then take this advice: solve the internal problem first. A relationship with God does not consist of the usual:

I believe in God in my own way

I go to church on Sundays

I'm a Christian

I grew up in church

I'm saved

A relationship with God consists of the usual requirements of any other relationship. For a mother to have a relationship with her daughter, she must talk to her, be a friend, understand her, get to know her needs, please her, sacrifice for her, make time for her, and invest in her.

If she doesn't do these things, she cannot complain that her daughter doesn't talk to her; it's just nonsense to think that you can have a relationship with someone just because of what you mean to that person.

Yes, God did give His Son for us so we could be saved, but that doesn't mean we're saved; it just means we can be saved. For us to be truly saved, we need to have a relationship with Him, the kind that fulfills all the natural requirements of any relationship.

Let's go over the list above in relation to a mother-daughter relationship:

I like my daughter in my own way

I spend two hours with her on Sundays

I pay her bills

I raised her

I'm her mother

Are these enough to have a relationship with your daughter? Of course not! Perhaps you craved for a relationship with your mother when you were growing up and you often rebelled just so you could get her to at least notice

A relationship with God consists of the usual requirements of any other relationship.

 The woman

you… just one of those things we do out of a need for a true relationship.

With God, it's different though; He's never unaware of how much we do or don't want Him. In fact, He's usually just waiting for us to say the word and invite Him in. But there's only so much He can do. If you only give Him two hours of your week, that's only how much you'll have of Him.

The V-Woman has a relationship with God and, because of this relationship, she fears Him. Many people don't understand what fearing God really means, apart from the fact that they fear losing their salvation and going to hell.

To fear God is to stay away from things that can interrupt your relationship with God. And that's a long list of things! Almost everything in this world is on this list because this world is getting further and further away from God. The closer to the darkness you get, the darker you'll get. The closer to the light you get, the lighter you'll get. It's common sense.

He's usually just waiting for us to say the word and invite Him in.

You can be the most amazing human being

and still be in the dark and subject to everything on that awful side of life. A woman who fears God puts her faith above everything else in her life, including friends, family, marriage, career, school, fun, money, looks, and success. And because of the way her priorities are handled, she shall be praised – not by people only, but mostly by God.

God's praise comes in different forms of happiness. You know when you're so proud of someone, when you feel so blessed by them, you love them for real, and you can't help but surprise them with something just to show them what they mean to you? That's what God does all the time.

He praises us when we're in the middle of world war III, giving us the ability to smile, laugh, have peace, and believe that better days are yet to come. Who else can do that except those who have a close relationship with God? He praises us when He fulfills our dreams in the most miraculous ways.

POOR AND DYING

The widow of Zarephath was praised by God in the most unorthodox way. Her story begins when God

sees her in particular, among all the other women and widows of her community, and sends His prophet Elijah her way just so a miracle can happen in her life:

> *Then the word of the LORD came to him, saying, "Arise, go to Zarephath, which belongs to Sidon, and dwell there. See, I have commanded a widow there to provide for you."*

(1 Kings 17:8,9)

God can be funny sometimes. As we read on, if there was one thing this widow could not do was provide!

> *And when he came to the gate of the city, indeed a widow was there gathering sticks. And he called to her and said, "Please bring me a little water in a cup, that I may drink." And as she was going to get it, he called to her and said, "Please bring me a morsel of bread in your hand."*
>
> *So she said, "As the LORD your God lives, I do not have bread, only a handful of flour in a bin, and a little oil in a jar; and see, I am gathering a couple of sticks*

that I may go in and prepare it for myself
and my son, that we may eat it, and die."

(1 Kings 17:10-12)

She was brutally honest with Elijah. Sometimes life takes the wrong turn and everything goes downhill. That's what happened to this widow. First, her husband dies leaving her alone to feed herself and child – remember that, in those days, women couldn't work. Then famine strikes the land, just to add salt to the wound... the woman was basically preparing her and her son's burial.

And here comes a strong man of God asking her for the only thing she had to survive one more day. No wonder she was detailed about the reason she was gathering sticks.

> *And Elijah said to her, "Do not fear; go*
> *and do as you have said, but make me*
> *a small cake from it first, and bring it to*
> *me; and afterward make some for yourself*
> *and your son. For*
> *thus says the LORD*

He (God) praises
us when we're in
the middle of
world war III...

God of Israel: 'The bin of flour shall not be used up, nor shall the jar of oil run dry, until the day the LORD sends rain on the earth.'" So she went away and did according to the word of Elijah; and she and he and her household ate for many days. The bin of flour was not used up, nor did the jar of oil run dry, according to the word of the LORD which He spoke by Elijah.

(1 Kings 17:13-16)

Talk about a miraculous turn of events! One minute she was poor and dying, the next she had enough to host Elijah as a guest in her house for many days and save her family, in the middle of national starvation.

It all comes down to that one little decision she made of just believing and obeying. She could have said, "No get out of here. I don't want to ever see you again." And if she had said that, we would have understood her; Elijah was indeed asking a little too much from a dying woman.

Sometimes life takes the wrong turn and everything goes downhill.

But that's how God works and will always work. No matter how much human beings change, God's ways will never change. He always gives you opportunities to use your faith and see results from it, but that's about all He'll do – give you opportunities and let you reap the consequences of your choices.

She chose to believe Elijah's word about God's power and obey it. She could have believed it but not have obeyed it either, just like many Christians do. They believe in the Bible, but they don't obey it. They won't wait until marriage to have sex, they won't tell the truth always, they won't be faithful at whatever cost. They're basically saying to God, "Get outta here! It's the 21st century. Everybody does it, and I have my needs."

The widow of Zarephath feared God and so she was praised. Her story was purposely included in God's Word, and not only that, she and her son did not die like most other families did. God came through for them in a miraculous way. Just one of those things He loves to do.

What has come between you and your faith in God?

What can you do to get rid of it?

How can you begin fearing God more?

The V woman

My Notes

_____
_____
_____
_____
_____
_____
_____
_____
_____
_____
_____
_____
_____
_____
_____
_____
_____
_____

She makes a difference

*Give her of the fruit of her hands, and let
her own works praise her in the gates.*

(Proverbs 31:31)

People can talk and write about a woman who has done so much in society, in government, or in her community, but she'll only be worthy of praise when her own works bring her praise. Anybody can do charity work nowadays, it's even fashionable, but it's usually about one's own image; it's done so they can look good. These are not the type of people that make a difference in the world.

If you want to make a difference in the world, you must have the audacity to be unpopular and controversial. The world is not praising those who do good to others, who are true role models, and who can portray God in their lives. Those are

considered fools. However, the world is praising those who are totally against God's ways. And that spirit has been infiltrating even churches to the point that many Christians themselves have begun to think that it's okay to sleep with your boyfriend, to do drugs, to party in clubs every Friday night and attend church on Sunday mornings. The world has made its way inside churches and nobody is doing anything about it. Pastors are only there to motivate people to keep on believing, no matter what kind of life they choose to live.

When we decide to stand up against this nonsense, we're practically crucified. That is why few people make a difference in this world, because most of them are just too worried about their own lives and reputation to go down that road.

You can't ever fully become this V-Woman if all you do is within your own reach. You may be a great mother, a perfect wife, and an extraordinary daughter, but if you don't reach out to

> You may be a great mother... but if you don't reach out to others outside your own little world, you'll still be an ordinary woman.

others outside your own little world, you'll still be an ordinary woman.

Let's consider what the Lord Jesus said about this: "Suppose one of you had a servant plowing or looking after the sheep. Would he say to the servant when he comes in from the field, 'Come along now and sit down to eat'? Would he not rather say, 'Prepare my supper, get yourself ready and wait on me while I eat and drink; after that you may eat and drink'? Would he thank the servant because he did what he was told to do? So you also, when you have done everything you were told to do, should say, 'We are unworthy servants; we have only done our duty'" (Luke 17:7-10 NIV).

All that you do at home, at work, in school, or in church is basically already expected of you. If you do it well, you're just doing what you're supposed to do. But when you do that AND you reach out to others while you're at it, THEN you're doing more than what you're asked to. THEN you're coming out of your comfort zone. THEN you're starting to make a difference in the world outside your own.

You reach out to others while the average woman couldn't care less about them. You expose your past and openly talk about how you've overcome it. You tell

them the truth, no matter how much it hurts. You are not double-minded about your faith in God. You base your life on His Word and you're transparent about this to everyone you know.

People who know me well know that I'm not spotlight material. I am at my best when I'm alone and I think that is probably something I inherited from my father. Don't get me wrong, I love being with my family and friends, but I do feel very comfortable when there's no one around and I can just sit and write. I am a naturally shy person and that is a fact I hate to admit. But in order for me to do everything I've done so far, I've had to sacrifice this lonely nature of mine, also known as shyness. I had to kill that will to be invisible and bring myself into the spotlight so I could make a difference in other people's lives. It's still very hard and people often judge me in all the wrong ways.

PROVERBS 18:1 SAYS IT ALL:

A man who isolates himself seeks his own desires; he rages against all wise judgment.

You can't make a difference in the world if you're seeking your own desire!

If you want to fulfill a dream, come out of your comfort zone and do what you don't feel like doing. It's not about what you feel like; it's about what you have to do. This is one of the top secrets of faith! You do without the need to feel like doing it.

This V-Woman verse above has a really nice twist to it. "Give her of the fruit of her hands," that is, let her rejoice with the outcome of her work; it's her right to have it. And then it says, "And let her own works praise her in the gates." In other words, the outcome of her work will be the one to praise her.

She's not boasting about herself, her achievements, her success, or the difference she has made in other people's lives. Instead, she's just rejoicing in them. That alone is a point of distinction between those who truly make a difference in the world and those who don't.

Our human nature is always looking for ways to boost our egos. When we're children, we want to tell everyone about the new toy we got. When we're teenag-

> If you want to fulfill a dream, come out of your comfort zone and do what you don't feel like doing.

ers, we want to be popular with everyone and be talked about as the one who does this and that. When we're dating, we want people to think how lucky we are for being loved by someone. When we're married, we want people to think we have this perfect life. When we have children, we want our children to be better than all the others... I think you get where I'm going here.

We want good things but they're all for our own ego, not for anyone else's benefit. That's where we fall.

You can only truly make a difference in your family, in your neighborhood, in your marriage, in your job, in your church, and in your world when you get rid of the above obsession with your own success; when you decide not to care about your ego and only care about others and their needs.

Once you begin making a difference outside your own life, you begin to enjoy it. The more you help others, the more you'll want to because the rewards you get from see-

You'll never have to boast about what you've done for others – they'll do that for you.

ing people benefiting from your life is just priceless. You'll never have to boast about what you've done for others – they'll do that for you. Your works will do the praising for you.

HOUSEWIFE AND ORDINARY

Jael is little known among the women in the Bible, but the little she did in her days was so great and honorable that God made sure her work was recorded in His Word.

She was a housewife, a common role in those days. But she was not limited by that role. She was a woman of courage; she took initiatives, and used opportunities; she knew exactly how to be a helper.

Those were days of war. Two important nations were coming against one another, and there she was, right in the middle of it. Even though her husband had decided not to affiliate his tribe with any of the two nations, he was giving too much information to the enemies of Israel. Jael had heard about Israel's battles and, most importantly, Israel's all powerful God; and so she could clearly see how her husband was making a big mistake.

The woman

One day, out of the blue, the war knocked on her door. Sisera, the army commander of the enemies of Israel came to her tent asking for some shelter. He was running away from the battle that had gone really badly for him. All his army was practically dead and the only way for their nation not to lose this war that day was for him to flee, get home safely, and make other plans to destroy Israel. Since Jael's husband had already given Sisera support, he must have felt that he could just go to their house and hide there for a while.

> *And Jael went out to meet Sisera, and said to him, "Turn aside, my lord, turn aside to me; do not fear." And when he had turned aside with her into the tent, she covered him with a blanket. Then he said to her, "Please give me a little water to drink, for I am thirsty." So she opened a jug of milk, gave him a drink, and covered him. And he said to her, "Stand at the door of the tent, and if any man comes and inquires of you, and says, 'Is there any man here?' you shall say, 'No.'"*

(Judges 4:18-20)

Here's Jael trying to pretend she's happy to see the enemy at her door. Sisera was a dangerous man, just like any man who battles against God. They can't be trusted; after all, they don't follow any good morals, but their own. Jael knew that if she'd not helped this man, she could have been killed by him, so she decided to be hospitable.

> *Then Jael, Heber's wife, took a tent peg and took a hammer in her hand, and went softly to him and drove the peg into his temple, and it went down into the ground; for he was fast asleep and weary. So he died. And then, as Barak pursued Sisera, Jael came out to meet him, and said to him, "Come, I will show you the man whom you seek." And when he went into her tent, there lay Sisera, dead with the peg in his temple.*
>
> (Judges 4:21,22)

Jael knew that if she'd not helped this man, she could have been killed by him, so she decided to be hospitable.

Sisera didn't even see his death coming! Jael wasn't a woman of war or of violence; she was simply a woman who chose to do what was right by God. She didn't care how disgusting and gross the whole hammer-down- a-peg-into-the-man's-temple would look; all she cared about was to end this nonsense against the people of God. Here she had the enemy of God sleeping in her own tent; the least she could do was to kill him!

It's interesting to read the next verse: "So on that day God subdued Jabin king of Canaan in the presence of the children of Israel. And the hand of the children of Israel grew stronger and stronger against Jabin king of Canaan, until they had destroyed Jabin king of Canaan" (Judges 4:23,24).

God is looking for influential women nowadays so He can win the variety of spiritual wars around us.

It was only on that day that God destroyed the enemies of His people. God used Jael, a woman, a housewife, a little nobody married to a man who didn't have the backbone to choose a side, to give His people victory once and for all.

Jael was a V-Woman who made a difference in Israel and in history. She also made a difference in her own life because that courageous attitude must have given her a whole new perspective on how valuable she was, regardless of who she was and what she did.

Her work praised her, for all of Israel now knew who Jael was – the woman God used to win the war.

God is looking for influential women nowadays so He can win the variety of spiritual wars around us. Here's a list of traits influential women usually have:

1. They're bold and courageous to stand out. Honestly, how can you influence others if you let your shyness stop you from ever doing anything new?

2. They're out there. They put themselves out there. Though most of them do it for the wrong reasons, it's still important to note that without putting yourself in front of everyone's eyes, it'll be impossible to ever be influential.

3. They excel at what they do. They aren't just good at it, they're the best! If you're simply a good student, good employee, good daughter, good moth-

The woman

er, or good wife, you can forget about ever influencing anybody. People look up to people who are better than them.

4. They are beautiful. This may sound vain but, honestly, does anybody listen to women who couldn't care less about their looks? Let's be honest, looks do attract people, so let's use it for God's glory.

What can you do to make a difference in your family?

What about your neighborhood, your workplace, your Church?

My Notes

*I*f you didn't skip through the whole book, you now have all the knowledge about what a V-Woman is about and how to become one. But knowledge alone is worthless if you don't start using it for your own benefit.

You've learned a lot and there's much to do in order to start implementing all of it, but don't dismay. Usually, there's so much to change that we tend to give up before we've even started. It's another common bad trait of us humans: Whenever we think we can't, we simply don't even try. Don't let yourself be entangled by that idea; instead, be wise and start working on your changes little by little.

Step 1. Look back at the end of each chapter and collect all your answers to the questions asked there.

Step 2. Add them to this next section of the book and prioritize them based on how important and urgent they are. See which trait is hurting you the most and decide to work on that one first. Put it at the top of the list.

Step 3. Add a deadline to each item you'll be working on. Don't think too little of yourself saying that you need a whole year to change something. But on the other hand, don't try to change everything in one week. Be realistic. You can probably change a lot in one month if you focus on one item alone that month.

Step 4. Once you can clearly see a change, go for the next item. If you still haven't changed as much as you wanted within your deadline, change your deadline – it's not the end of the world and you can still do it.

Step 5. Reward yourself for each achievement. Make it a point to do that every time; it may sound childish, but it's not. We

See which trait is hurting you the most and decide to work on that one first.

all love to be rewarded sometimes, especially if we feel good about ourselves.

Once you finish all the steps to becoming a V-Woman and you can say with much happiness in your heart that you've become one, bless someone else with this book – you may want to lend your own or simply buy another and give it as a gift to someone you know who would greatly benefit from it.

I'd also love to hear from you. Please do stop by my daily blog www.cristianecardoso.com and leave me a comment about how this book has blessed you. I'll enter your e-mail address (if you provide it) into my own personal database of V-Women and from time to time, e-mail you more updates on how to keep on growing as a V-Woman.

The woman

My Notes

PRINTED AND BOUND BY
Clays Ltd, St Ives plc